the Olive Tree

GROWTH ▨▨▨▨   LIGHT GROWTH ▭

YEAR BOOK OF THE OLIVE OIL ASSOCIATION OF AMERICA, INC.

Mediterranean Specialties
for the Modern Cook

Mediterranean Specialties for the Modern Cook

CON AMOR Y CON SAVOR

Compiled and tested by

Esther B. Cory

Thomas Y. Crowell Company

New York, Established 1834

DESIGNED BY LAUREL WAGNER

Manufactured in the United States of America
by The Colonial Press Inc., Clinton, Massachusetts

LIBRARY OF CONGRESS CATALOG CARD NO. 63-15094

First Printing

This edition of
Mediterranean Specialties for the Modern Cook
has been especially prepared for
Filippo Berio Olive Oil, Inc.

Introduction

In this book you will find dishes from the countries that rim the sun-drenched shores of the Mediterranean —Spain, Italy, Greece, Israel, Tunis, and Turkey. Many of them have never before been published. These are recipes that the Sephardic Jews brought with them to many countries of the Mediterranean centuries ago; the recipes have been modified during the years, to reflect, in part, the traditions of the new countries. Hence, these recipes are different from similar ones associated with Mediterranean cuisine. They are simple to prepare and have been chosen with the modern cook in mind. They will tempt the fussiest gourmet and become staple dishes for family meals as they have in our home and in the homes of our friends. With equal grace they will sit with the most sumptuous dinner-party menu. In addition you will have the satisfaction of knowing that this type of cooking preserves the maximum vitamin content and food value.

The recipes given here can accompany steak, ham, or even the ubiquitous hamburger and make what might have been a routine meal interesting and still easy on the cook. The recipes for vegetables, rice, and vermicelli are particularly appropriate in this respect.

Mediterranean cuisine is based on the regional abundance of pure olive oil, tomatoes, and green vegetables (all of which are now available to the American kitchen as well). To the Mediterranean cook, fresh straight leaf parsley, also known as Italian parsley, and oregano are musts, for the flavor of parsley or oregano, diffused through meat or fish, lifts the taste from flat to exquisite. Next in importance are fresh celery leaves. This leaf needs to be appreciated and used more by Americans. It imparts an unusual and delicious note of variety to many dishes. Then, of course, there is dill, basil, rosemary, mint, and tarragon. With these one graduates from the science of cooking to the art of cooking.

While these are simple recipes, they are not effortless; a little loving care is necessary and will reap pleasure for you, your family, and guests.

- Select a good olive oil. Taste it if you are not a regular olive oil user. It should have a delicate flavor with a pleasant bouquet.
- Select fresh vegetables. When cooking them keep an eye on the time so they will not overcook.
- Use olive oil and condiments discreetly as demonstrated in this collection of recipes.

As my *suegra,* or mother-in-law, used to maintain: You must nourish your dear ones *con amor y con savor*—with love and with taste.

BON APPETIT!

Acknowledgments

To all of those whose enthusiastic help has made this book a reality I would like to express my gratitude: to my sisters-in-law, Victoria Corri, Rose Franco, and Suzanne Amateau, whose culinary skill is matched by extraordinary patience and generosity in demonstrating the preparation of many of these Mediterranean dishes; to my brothers-in-law, Jacques Corri, Victor Cory, and Elias Cory, and to Dr. Morris Amateau, who have eagerly undertaken to answer any questions pertaining to Greek and Turkish customs or language. Also I must thank my American sisters-in-law, Hortense and Irma Cory, who became experts in analyzing and preparing Sephardic, Greek, and Turkish dishes.

I must acknowledge my daughter, Ellen Cory Epstein, who has helped to make this book useful for the young and busy housewife who enjoys fine food, and my son, David, who consumes our special dishes with such heartwarming gusto!

In this circle I must include Mrs. Inez Rissotto who has reinforced me with her infinite patience in typewriting these recipes; as well as our friends, who have brought delight to our home and sought these recipes.

E.B.C.

A NOTE FROM THE AUTHOR

I cannot stress strongly enough the need to use a top quality olive oil in the preparation of the recipes in this book. I have used Filippo Berio Italian Olive Oil when testing these recipes and recommend it to you without reservation.

Contents

Notes and Suggestions

A light stock imparts such a distinctive flavor to so many of the dishes in the Mediterranean cuisine that it is regarded as an essential ingredient in preparing rice, vermicelli, and various vegetables. A quart of stock should always be on hand in the refrigerator. It may be prepared from beef, beef bones, or poultry giblets.

CHICKEN OR BEEF STOCK

Place chicken giblets or ½ pound of beef (neck or chuck) in a saucepan with a quart of water and a teaspoon of salt. Cover, and allow to simmer 25 to 60 minutes, adding enough water to produce a quart of stock. Keep stock in refrigerator for use when needed.

When frying with olive oil, to obtain best results proceed as follows. Pour the required amount of oil in a cool pan. Start with low heat until the oil is warm. Then increase to desired intensity. This prevents oil from smoking.

Several of the recipes call for heating the olive oil till it browns a cube of bread, then cooling the oil before adding stock or water (so that it won't spatter). The preheated oil gives a special flavor to grains such as rice and bulgur.

Heating or braising pieces of meat or eggplant in hot oil before cooking not only seals in the juices, but the film of olive oil imparts an additional subtle flavor to the food.

When olive oil is used in the preparation of turkey stuffing or for rubbing the bird, the resulting flavor distinguishes the offering and transforms run-of-the-mill turkey into a rare gastronomical treat.

Poultry stuffing can be further enhanced by using, generously, Italian parsley and chestnuts, and by using half white and half seeded rye bread. The addition of caraway seeds and onion sautéed in a fine olive oil embellish the flavor to a surprising degree.

When a recipe calls for minced onion, cut the onion in half across the center. Then, across the flat surface of one of the halves, make cuts ⅛ to ¼ inch deep and ¼ inch apart. Turn the onion and make cuts at right angles. Slice the onion to the depth of the cuts, allowing the small pieces to fall into a dish. Repeat this procedure until you have the quantity desired.

To mince parsley, first wash it and shake it dry; then, holding a bunch of about four stalks in one hand, cut it at intervals of ¼ inch with a paring knife. Parsley cut this way retains its maximum aroma and improves the texture of the mixture in which it is used.

Meat should be removed from the refrigerator a half hour before cooking it. The meat should be at about room temperature.

Rice is as important a feature in the Mediterranean menu as roast beef or apple pie is in the American menu. A properly prepared platter of rice is the climax of the meal and the test of the skill of the cook. The rice must be firm but tender with each grain separate. Having watched my family for years, I noted how my sisters-in-law guarded certain saucepans for rice as if they were enchanted. Eventually I realized that the saucepan which produced the desired result had to have certain proportions. The saucepan for making the perfect rice has to have a wide base and be fairly shallow. A saucepan, a pudding pan, or a casserole 4 to 5 inches deep will consistently produce the desired rice. This proportion was the secret of the spell!

To cook one cup of rice a pan with a base of 6 inches is adequate.

For 2 to 3 cups of rice a pan with a span of 8 to 9 inches is required.

In Italy, spaghetti or the pasta is served at the beginning of the meal; the order of service is:

> Antipasto
> Pasta
> Fish or Meat
> Vegetable
> Dessert

In Greece and Turkey, the order is different. It is:

> Hors d'oeuvres
> Salad
> Entree and Vegetables
> Rice or Bulgur
> Dessert

Appetizers and Side Dishes

Fried Almonds

Almonds fried in a fine olive oil have an entirely different and a superior flavor to almonds fried in a completely bland oil.

Blanch ½ pound almonds and drain them on paper. Heat olive oil, ½ inch deep, in a small skillet till it browns a small round of bread. Add the almonds, cook till they are golden brown and drain them on brown paper. Salt them and serve them warm or cold. Retain the olive oil, since it can be used for other cooking or frying. Fried almonds may be kept for future use in a sealed jar stored in a cool, dry place. SERVES 6.

Salted Roasted Walnuts or Almonds

    2 pounds walnuts or almonds in shells
    1 tablespoon salt

Preheat oven to 375°F. Warm nuts in a shallow pan. Dissolve salt in ¼ cup water and sprinkle it over the warm nuts. Let the salted nuts roast until water is evaporated and the nuts are dry. Remove from oven. Serve cool.

Anchovies and Pimientos

    1 4-ounce can roasted pimientos
    1 2-ounce can rolled anchovies
    2 tablespoons olive oil
    1 tablespoon wine vinegar

Cut pimientos into 1½-inch squares. Drain the oil from the can and place one anchovy on each square of pimiento. Blend the olive oil and vinegar thoroughly and pour over anchovies and pimientos. Serve on squares of crisp bread.

Garlic Almond Paste

This exquisite dish was served to us on the Island of Büyükada, one of the Princes Islands in the Sea of Marmora, Turkey. It is best served with fish or light meat.

    1 slice of white bread
    ½ cup blanched almonds
    1 bitter almond
      Sliver of garlic

Moisten bread; squeeze out excess water. Add the remaining ingredients; pound the mixture or grind in a small mill till smooth.

Boiled Artichokes

    4 artichokes
    3 tablespoons salt
    2 tablespoons vinegar

Wash artichokes. Add salt and vinegar to 4 quarts of
boiling water. Cook artichokes 20 to 30 minutes till
leaves pull out easily. Drain, cool, and serve with Vinaigrette Sauce. SERVES 4.

VINAIGRETTE SAUCE FOR BOILED ARTICHOKES

    ½ teaspoon pepper
    ½ teaspoon salt
       Touch of tabasco sauce
    ½ teaspoon English or French mustard
    3 tablespoons olive oil
    1 tablespoon cider vinegar
    2 tablespoons beef consommé
    1 teaspoon minced onion
    ½ teaspoon minced garlic

Blend seasonings with olive oil; add vinegar and con-
sommé. Stir thoroughly. Lastly, blend in onion and
garlic.

Jerusalem Artichokes [*Toombala*]
                              TURKEY

    1 pound Jerusalem artichokes
    2 tablespoons olive oil

3 tablespoons tomato sauce
½ teaspoon salt
1 teaspoon lemon juice

Scrape and wash artichokes. Bring 2 cups of water, olive oil, and tomato sauce to boil. Add salt, artichokes, and lemon juice. Cook till tender, about 40 minutes. Brown the artichokes under broiler before serving. SERVES 6.

Artichokes, Smyrna Style [*Enginar*]

Artichokes prepared in this manner have an entirely different flavor from the vegetable when cooked whole. Select green, heavy artichokes, preferably small ones. If only large artichokes are available, discard the large outer leaves.

4 artichokes
2 lemons
2 tablespoons olive oil
1 teaspoon salt

Fill a large, deep pot with 2 quarts water, to contain the artichokes as they are being prepared. Squeeze the lemons, retaining the juice and adding the rinds to the water.

Remove the coarse outer leaves, working around until the leaves that are whitish are reached. With a large knife, cut each artichoke in half, cut off the tough part of the stem and the thorny part of the leaves. With a corer, scoop out the chokes. Immediately drop the hearts into the large pot of water. The rinds will prevent the artichokes from turning black.

In a shallow pan (3 to 4 inches deep), bring 4 cups of water and the olive oil to a boil. Add the salt, artichokes, and lemon juice. Cover with large lettuce leaves or the pan lid. Cook briskly till the hearts are tender and most of the liquid has evaporated. This should take 30 to 45 minutes. If necessary, add more water during the cooking. Remove the artichokes when tender. Let liquid boil down until the consistency of a thin gravy.

Serve the artichokes with the sauce at room temperature. When properly prepared, the artichoke hearts are a lovely pale green. SERVES 6.

Green Bean Salad [*Fagiolini*]

ITALY

1   pound green beans
1   teaspoon salt
2   tablespoons olive oil
3   tablespoons lemon juice or cider vinegar

Wash beans, snap off stems, and add beans to ¾ cup boiling water; add salt and cook till tender, 10 to 20 minutes. Cool and drain the beans. Blend the olive oil and lemon thoroughly and pour over the beans. Serve cool as an appetizer. SERVES 6.

Kidney Bean Salad

¾   cup canned dried beans
½   cup minced parsley
1   small onion, minced, or 3 scallions
2   tablespoons vinegar

3 tablespoons olive oil
Salt and pepper

Boil kidney beans till tender, about 30 minutes. Drain
and cool the beans. Blend the remaining ingredients well,
adding salt and pepper to taste. Pour over cool beans.
Serve as an appetizer. SERVES 4.

Beet Relish [*Kuchundooria*]

TURKEY

Beets prepared this way are used as a relish with meat.
Wash beets thoroughly. Top the beets, leaving 1 inch of
the stems to retain color. Retain some of the stems that
were cut off. Cover the beets with boiling water and
cook till tender. Young beets will cook in 30 to 60 minutes, depending on size. Place the cooked beets in a pan
of cold water and slip off their skins. Cut the beets in
quarters and put them in a bowl or jar with one medium-
sized onion which has been quartered and sliced. Add
cider vinegar blended with double the amount of boiled
water to cover and 1 teaspoon of salt. Serve cold as a
relish with chicken or meat.

Cucumber Relish with Bread Dressing [*Ajada*]

SMYRNA

I should call this Cucumber in a Drift of Snow. As simple as this dish is, it has always intrigued our guests.

They like to guess its ingredients and are happy to believe it is the caviar of a very well-born and rare fish with occult powers!

   1 large cucumber
   2 thick chunks stale white bread from which
         crust has been removed
   ½ clove garlic
   2 tablespoons olive oil or just enough to make
         a paste
   1 tablespoon lemon juice

Rub bread together till you have 4 tablespoons of fine crumbs. Mash with garlic, olive oil, and lemon juice to a paste. Peel cucumber, slice it into ¼-inch rounds, and chill them. Add 1 tablespoon of cold water to the paste and spread on chilled cucumber slices. Refrigerate till ready to serve. SERVES 4.

Green Pepper Relish

   4 medium green peppers
   2 tablespoons olive oil
   1 tablespoon vinegar
      Pinch of sugar
      Clove of garlic, split

Wash peppers and remove stems and seeds. Cook in small amount of boiling water about 8 minutes or till tender. Remove skin, drain, cut in strips, and put in clean jar. Add 2 parts olive oil to 1 part vinegar _ tablespoons cool boiled water, sugar, and garlic.

Green Pepper Appetizers I [*Peperoni Verdi*]

ITALY

Green peppers
Olive oil

Remove seeds and cut peppers into ¾-inch strips. In hot olive oil ¼ inch deep, sauté peppers until tender. Drain on brown paper and serve hot.

Green Pepper Appetizers II

  6 green peppers
  3 tablespoons olive oil
  1 teaspoon capers
12 black olives, sliced
  4 tablespoons lemon juice

Cut peppers in halves and remove seeds. Cook in small amount of water until tender. Drain. Sauté in olive oil. Drain. Add capers, olives, and lemon juice. Toss well. Serve at room temperature.

Carrot Vinaigrette

Cut carrots in discs or strips. Cook in small quantity of boiling salted water. Drain liquid; blend it with equal amount of cider vinegar. Add salt to taste. Pour over carrots. Serve cool.

Cauliflower Patties [*Keftez*]

    3 cups cooked cauliflower
    2 eggs
    1 cup flour
    ¾ cup milk
    ⅓ cup olive oil
    ⅓ cup tomato sauce
       Salt and pepper
    1 tablespoon grated Parmesan cheese
       (optional)

Slice cauliflower scant ½ inch thick. Blend eggs, flour, and milk, beating well to make a thin batter. Dip slices of cauliflower in the batter. Fry the slices in hot olive oil till they are golden brown. Place patties in a shallow casserole.

Heat the tomato sauce, ⅓ cup water, seasoning, and 2 tablespoons of the olive oil in which the patties were fried. Pour this sauce over the patties in the casserole. Sprinkle with grated Parmesan cheese and brown lightly under broiler. SERVES 6.

Turnip Vinaigrette, Arab Style

My husband and I came upon this dish in a Druse (Arab) inn—on a hilltop several kilometres outside of Haifa. Never before had we enjoyed eating turnip as we did when it was prepared in this fashion.

Wash, peel, and cut turnips into strips or slices. Cover with boiling water, adding 1 teaspoon of salt to a quart of water. Cook for 20 minutes or till tender. Drain, reserving ¾ cup liquid. Blend liquid with ⅜ to ¾ cup cider vinegar and a pinch of sugar. Pour over turnips. Serve cool.

Stuffed Grape Leaves [*Yaprak*]

TURKEY

20 to 22 grape leaves (canned, Greek style)
¾ cup rice (short grain)
 1 cup minced parsley
 1 large onion, minced
    Salt and pepper
¼ cup olive oil
 2 tablespoons lemon juice

Pour boiling water over leaves and soak them for 5 minutes. Then soak them in cold water. Drain and separate the leaves.

Mix the rice with parsley, onion, and seasoning. Let stand for 15 minutes. Drain off liquid. Then place a heaping teaspoon of the mixture in the center of each leaf. Turn left side over it, then right side; roll and arrange firmly in a shallow pan or casserole. If leaves tear, overlap two parts and place mixture in center.

Pour olive oil and lemon juice on top. Add ½ cup water and simmer for 45 minutes until water is absorbed and rice is tender. Serve at room temperature, with yoghurt, if desired. SERVES 6.

Spinach Stalks Vinaigrette

Boil spinach stalks with just enough water to cover till tender. Add ½ clove garlic and season to taste. Serve with Lemon and Olive Oil Dressing.

Onion Rings

    1 pound Bermuda or Spanish onions
    2 eggs
   ½ cup flour
   ¼ cup milk
   ½ teaspoon salt
      Olive oil

Slice onions in ¼-inch slices, crosswise, and separate into rings. Prepare a light batter by beating eggs, then adding flour, milk, and salt; it should have the consistency of heavy cream. Stir in a few rings at a time till thoroughly coated. Fry in deep hot olive oil until golden brown and crisp. Remove and drain on brown paper. Serve hot. If necessary keep hot on a platter in oven. SERVES 6.

Calf's Brains Vinaigrette

    1 pair calf brains
    1 tablespoon vinegar
   ½ teaspoon salt
    1 scant tablespoon lemon juice
    2 tablespoons olive oil

Salt and pepper
1 teaspoon small capers
2 teaspoons minced parsley

Remove brains from refrigerator, let stand at room temperature for 20 minutes. Immerse in cold water and remove the membrane.

Place brains in a saucepan containing boiling water to cover, to which 1 tablespoon vinegar and ½ teaspoon of salt have been added. Cook for 15 minutes, leaving the brains whole. Remove, drain, and let cool.

Blend thoroughly the lemon juice, olive oil, seasoning, and 4 mashed capers. Pour mixture over the brains. Garnish with the rest of capers and minced parsley. Serve cold. SERVES 4.

Chicken Giblet Hors d'oeuvres

Giblets and neck of chicken
2 tablespoons diced onion
2 tablespoons olive oil
Salt and pepper
1 tablespoon wine vinegar

Boil the giblets and neck of chicken from 20 to 40 minutes, according to tenderness of gizzard. Pick off meat from the neck and dice this meat and the giblets. Fry onion in hot olive oil till limp. Add the giblets and neck meat, continuing to fry for about 3 minutes. Add the seasoning to taste and stir in the vinegar. Serve hot on toast or crackers. SERVES 6.

Simple to prepare, but a pleasing surprise to the palate.

Chicken Liver Paté

    1 medium-sized onion
    2 tablespoons olive oil
    2 fresh chicken livers
    1 egg, boiled 5 minutes
       Salt and pepper

Slice onion, fry in hot olive oil till a light brown. Add
chicken livers and fry for about 2 minutes on each side
until cooked but not overdone. Drain and transfer to a
wooden bowl. Chop thoroughly. Add boiled egg, 1 teaspoon of the olive oil which was used for frying, and
seasoning, and mix until it is a smooth paste. Serve cool
on crackers or wedges of bread. SERVES 6.

Greek Fish Roe [*Tarama*]

    2 slices dry white bread
   ¼ teaspoon minced garlic (optional)
    2 tablespoons bottled tarama
  1½ tablespoons lemon juice
   ½ cup olive oil

Trim bread and sprinkle lightly with water. In a bowl
mash bread and blend with garlic (if used), tarama, and
half the lemon juice. Stir in the olive oil one tablespoon at
a time. When all the olive oil is absorbed add the rest of
the lemon juice. The texture should be that of thick
mayonnaise. Chill and serve on squares of bread or with
bland crackers.

   If an electric blender is used, turn off every few
moments to prevent separation from excessive agitation.

Soups

Vegetable Soup [*Menestra de Verduras*]

ESTREMADURA, SPAIN

½ pound potatoes, peeled and quartered
2 onions, sliced
½ cup olive oil
3 cups beef stock
½ pound green beans, cooked
½ pound spinach, cut in small pieces
3 carrots, cooked
1 green pepper, diced
1 teaspoon cumin seed
1 clove garlic
2 tablespoons parsley, minced
½ teaspoon basil
1 hard-cooked egg yolk

Sauté potatoes and onions in olive oil, stirring well. When potato is browned, cover with a small amount of beef stock. Cook till potatoes are tender. Add the remaining vegetables and stock.

Pound and make a paste of cumin seed, garlic, parsley, basil, the egg yolk and a little water. Add this paste to the vegetable mixture. Serve hot. SERVES 6.

Small artichoke hearts previously cooked may also be added. If leftover vegetables are used for this soup, they may be added to the beef stock shortly before serving, allowing just enough time for the vegetables to heat through.

Juanita Corchero, Mérida, Spain

Chicken Broth

1   4-pound fowl
    Salt
1   carrot
2   stalks of celery or dried celery root
    Onion (optional)
    Parsley leaves

Wash and disjoint chicken. Salt and let stand an hour or even overnight. Cover with 3 quarts water and bring to a boil. Cover tightly and let simmer for 2 hours or until meat is tender but not soft. Add vegetables and parsley and cook for ½ hour longer. Remove chicken, refrigerate and serve cool with mayonnaise. Strain and skim broth.

Broth may be served clear with parsley, noodles, boiled rice, or boiled spinach, or as Soup à la Reine, below. SERVES 6.

Soup à la Reine [*Avgolemono*]

GREECE

¾ tablespoon lemon juice, more or less
    according to taste
4 cups chicken broth
4 egg yolks

Add lemon juice to hot Chicken Broth. Pour mixture gradually over beaten egg yolks, stirring constantly. Serve immediately. If necessary, keep warm in top of double boiler. SERVES 4.

Lentil Soup [*Sopa de Lentejas*]

SMYRNA

1 onion, diced
2 tablespoons olive oil
4 cups beef stock
1 cup lentils
¼ cup tomato sauce
  Salt

Stock may be prepared by boiling beef bones and coarse meat from 45 minutes to 3 hours, thus extracting all the nutrients from the bones. Carrot and celery stalk may be added the last half hour.

Sauté the onion in the olive oil. Cool. Add 4 cups of strained stock, bring mixture to a boil, add the lentils and tomato sauce. Cook for about 45 minutes or till tender and then add salt. Serve hot. SERVES 6.

Marrow Bean Soup [*Habas Calduldas*]
ANCIENT ANDALUCÍA, SPAIN

¾ cup marrow beans
2 tablespoons olive oil
1 medium onion, sliced
2 marrow bones, or chunk of soup meat
½ cup tomato sauce
¾ teaspoon salt

Pick over beans; soak them overnight in cool water to cover or boil 2 minutes and let stand 1 hour in the hot water. In a small skillet heat olive oil; sauté onion till pale gold. Transfer to 2-quart pot, add 1 quart water, bones, tomato sauce, and beans. Cook briskly for 40 minutes. When tender, add salt. The beans should be tender but not falling apart and the liquid thick as a purée. Serve hot. SERVES 4.

Canned marrow beans may be used. They are all ready when drained to be combined with the onion, tomato sauce, and stock.

Pea Bean Soup

1 cup dried pea beans
1 pound escarole
1 clove garlic
4 tablespoons olive oil

Soak beans in water to cover overnight or boil 2 minutes and let stand 1 hour; then cook until tender. Cook escarole in small amount of water until tender. Reserve liquid, adding water if necessary to make 1 cup. Combine beans and escarole, bring to a boil, and reduce heat. Add garlic, olive oil, and 1 cup of liquid in which escarole was cooked. Simmer until blended. Discard garlic. SERVES 6.

Fish Soup, Malaga Style
[*Sopa de Rapa*]

This soup supplemented by salad is a meal in itself. You might use codfish, haddock, halibut, or hake.

       1 pound fish
      12 almonds
       1 tablespoon olive oil
       1 slice bread
       2 medium tomatoes, diced
       2 cups fish stock
          Salt
      ¼ teaspoon pepper
      ¼ teaspoon paprika

Poach fish in water to cover. Drain, reserving 2 cups stock. Blanch and sauté almonds in olive oil. Remove almonds and sauté the bread and tomatoes in the same oil. Add to fish stock. Whirl almonds in the blender or pound to a paste with the bread and tomatoes and then add to the fish stock mixture. Season. Serve hot over 2-inch squares of fish. SERVES 4.

Anita Lozano, Málaga

Gazpacho

1 onion, diced
1 large green pepper, seeded and chopped
8 ripe tomatoes, peeled and chopped
2 cucumbers, peeled and chopped
1 clove of garlic, peeled and mashed
2 teaspoons salt
½ teaspoon paprika (optional)
4 tablespoons olive oil
3 tablespoons wine vinegar
1 slice of bread, moistened

First Method: Combine half the vegetables with garlic, salt, and paprika. Put in a blender.

Mix the olive oil, vinegar, and 2 cups cold water. Put half in the blender. Run the blender until the vegetables are smoothly blended. Add the bread. Remove mixture from blender. Repeat the process with the remaining chopped vegetables and the rest of the liquid. Combine the two batches. Chill until very cold, but not so cold that the olive oil hardens. Taste for seasoning; add more if desired. Pour into chilled bouillon cups. At the table offer toasted croutons, diced cucumber, scallions, and green pepper.

Second Method: (As given by the Maître of the Andalucía Palace Hotel, Seville, Spain.) Cut into small pieces the onion, green pepper, tomatoes, and garlic, and mix all in an earthenware bowl. Pound for 5 minutes. When they become a paste add a bit of bread (previously

SOUPS   23

soaked in water), the olive oil, vinegar, and 2 cups very
cold water. Put the mixture through a coarse strainer.
Chill, and serve with a garnish of chopped tomatoes,
green pepper, and cucumber. SERVES 6 TO 8.

Sorrel Soup

    1   pound sorrel or ½ pound sorrel and ½
            pound spinach
    1   teaspoon salt
        White of 1 egg, beaten till foamy
            (optional)
    ½   cucumber, diced
    4   scallions, chopped
    1   hard-cooked egg
        Cream or sour cream (optional)

Wash sorrel leaves and drain. Discard stems, retaining
half inch, if desired. Bring 6 cups water to a boil, add
sorrel and salt and cook for 3 minutes. Remove leaves.
Chop or put in a blender with a small amount of the
liquid. Do not chop too fine. Return leaves to liquid.
Chill and stir in the beaten white of egg if it is being
used. Add cucumber, scallions, and hard-cooked egg put
through a coarse strainer. Serve with sweet or sour
cream, if desired. SERVES 4 TO 6.

Eggs and Omelets

Eggs, Cuban Style
[*Huevos Cubanos*]
ANDALUCÍA, SPAIN

    1 plantain or 1 banana (not too ripe)
    2 tablespoons olive oil
    2 eggs
       Pinch of salt
    ⅓ cup cooked rice
    ½ cup tomato sauce (see below)

The plantain is more fibrous than the usual type of banana. It is now being more widely used here in the United States and can be purchased at international food stores.

Peel and cut banana in half lengthwise. Brown lightly in hot olive oil in skillet. Then drop eggs into pan, keeping yolks whole. Sprinkle with salt and let cook on lowered heat until white is firm. Serve hot with the cooked rice topped with Tomato Sauce. SERVES 2.

TOMATO SAUCE

2 tablespoons olive oil
½ cup strained canned plum tomatoes or 1 cup
       canned tomato sauce
   Salt and pepper

This should be prepared in advance. In a small skillet
heat the olive oil until it browns a small piece of bread.
Discard bread and add the tomatoes or tomato sauce
and seasoning to the olive oil. Let simmer till well blended
and the consistency of a purée. Serve hot over the rice. If
desired, brown a half clove of garlic before adding the
tomatoes.

Eggs Poached in Tomato Sauce
[*Huevos en Tomate*]

SMYRNA

3 tablespoons olive oil
1 clove garlic, cut in half lengthwise
¾ cup strained Italian tomatoes or tomato sauce
¼ teaspoon salt
   Freshly ground pepper to taste
1 teaspoon crumbled dried mushroom (optional)
¼ teaspoon thyme or basil
3 eggs

Heat half the olive oil in 8-inch frying pan until it
browns a small piece of bread. Add garlic. When brown,

remove. Let olive oil cool, then add strained tomatoes, salt, and pepper. Let simmer 10 to 15 minutes. Add the rest of the olive oil, mushroom, and thyme or basil. Stir until thickened and well blended. Drop the eggs into the sauce, being careful not to break the yolks. Stir the whites with the sauce gently around the yolks until they are cooked and until the yolks are the desired consistency. Serve hot on toast. SERVES 3.

This is a good Sunday-night supper dish.

Parmesan Cheese Omelet

ITALY

3 eggs
¼ teaspoon salt
Dash of pepper
1 tablespoon bread crumbs
2 tablespoons grated Parmesan cheese
2 tablespoons milk or cream
2 tablespoons olive oil

Beat eggs, add salt and pepper, bread crumbs, cheese, and enough milk or cream to make the mixture smooth but not watery. In a 6-inch skillet heat olive oil gently. When warm, add mixture, beating lightly before pouring into pan. As omelet begins to cook, rotate the pan so that the heat browns the outer edge of omelet. When the underside is browned, turn the omelet over with a spatula. Move pan around until this side is browned. Serve hot with marmalade or currant jam. SERVES 3.

Eggs and Sliced Cheese, Greek Style

    2 tablespoons olive oil
    4 slices Kash Kaval cheese, Provolone, or any
        well-cured hard cheese, about 2½
        inches square
    4 eggs
    ¼ teaspoon salt
      Pepper to taste
    ½ lemon

Warm olive oil on low heat. Add slices of cheese. As soon
as cheese begins to soften, break eggs into pan, keeping
yolks whole. Add salt and pepper. Cook slowly until
white of egg is cooked to desired texture. Squeeze lemon
over eggs, removing seeds. Allow to cook extra half
minute.

With a spatula lift egg and cheese onto toast covered with the olive oil and lemon mixture instead of
butter. Serve immediately. SERVES 4.

A piquant Sunday breakfast or brunch dish.

Chive Omelet

    2 eggs
    1 tablespoon milk
    ¼ teaspoon salt
      Pinch of pepper
    2 tablespoons minced chives
    2 tablespoons olive oil

Beat eggs lightly, add milk, salt, pepper, and chives. Heat

olive oil in skillet. When it browns a small piece of bread, pour in the egg mixture. While cooking, draw edges toward center with knife or narrow spatula as they set. Fold and serve on hot platter. SERVES 2.

Omelet Fines Herbes

For the Omelet Fines Herbes, follow recipe for Chive Omelet substituting ½ thyme and ½ parsley flakes for the corresponding amount of chives.

Mushroom Omelet

¼ pound (or one 4-ounce can) small mushrooms
4 tablespoons butter or olive oil
3 eggs, separated
1 tablespoon cream
½ teaspoon salt
  Dash of black pepper

If you use fresh mushrooms, wash thoroughly and drain on towel. Sauté either fresh or canned mushrooms in 2 tablespoons olive oil or butter for 5 minutes.

Meanwhile beat egg yolks with cream, salt, and pepper till very light. Beat egg whites till stiff but not dry. Add the beaten yolks to the whites, blending thoroughly. Heat remaining olive oil or butter in an 8-inch frying pan on low heat. When warm, add the egg mixture, cooking slowly 5 to 10 minutes. When the eggs are well set, place the mushrooms over half, and with two large spatulas fold the omelet over the mushrooms. Serve hot. SERVES 3.

Fish and Fish Sauces

Fish that is absolutely fresh can be palatable and subtle even with the simplest cooking. Poached fish is satisfying served with lemon, olive oil, and freshly ground pepper. Also, removed from the bones and blended with Olive Oil Mayonnaise, it provides a true repast.

Fish Suitable for:

Poaching	*Baking and Broiling*	*Frying*
Bass	Bass	Butterfish
Cod	Bluefish	Cod steaks and fillets
Halibut	Cod steaks	
Salmon	Flounder	Flounder fillet
Haddock	Mackerel	Salmon steak
Scrod	Halibut steaks	Haddock fillet
	Salmon steaks	
	Weakfish	

Poached Fish I

On our last trip around the world some of the most delicious meals we savored in Turkey, on one of the

Princes Islands, and in Lisbon, Portugal, consisted of poached fish. In both places the method of cooking was identical. Fresh fish was poached in water with lemon, olive oil, and parsley, and served cool, with additional lemon and olive oil to taste. Of course, the olive oil used must be smooth, sweet, and fragrant.

> 1 tablespoon lemon juice
> 2 sprigs of parsley
> 1 teaspoon of salt
>   Pepper to taste
> 2 pounds fish

Place 1 quart water, lemon juice, parsley, salt, and pepper in shallow pan or oval fish pan and bring mixture to boil. Let simmer for 5 minutes till well blended. Add fish, let cook 10 to 15 minutes till flesh flakes easily with a fork but is still firm. Transfer to platter. Serve with Lemon and Olive Oil Sauce or with Olive Oil Mayonnaise. SERVES 6.

In Lisbon a small young onion is added to the stock.

Poached Fish II

> 2 pounds fish
> 1 tablespoon salt
> 2 tablespoons wine vinegar or lemon juice
>   Salt to taste
> ¼ teaspoon pepper
> 2 tablespoons diced onion
> 2 tablespoons diced carrot
> 2 tablespoons diced celery

Sprinkle fish with 1 tablespoon salt and let stand for one hour or more. Wash thoroughly. In saucepan mix together 2 cups water, vinegar or lemon juice, salt, pepper, and vegetables, and simmer till blended. Add fish and let cook till flesh is cooked but firm, and flakes easily. Place on platter.

Serve with Lemon and Olive Oil Sauce, with Mustard Sauce, or with mayonnaise. SERVES 6.

Poached Fish with Lemon and Egg Sauce

    2   pounds salmon or salmon trout
        Juice and grated rind of 1 lemon
    2   egg yolks
    ½   teaspoon sugar
    1   cup strained hot fish stock
        Salt to taste
    1   teaspoon minced parsley
    2   bay leaves

Follow directions for Poached Fish I or II, reserving stock. When fish is done, arrange on platter and set aside to cool.

Mix juice and grated rind of lemon with well-beaten yolks and sugar. Gradually stir into this the hot fish stock. Cook in top of double boiler until thick, stirring constantly. Add salt, parsley, and whole bay leaves. Chill and pour over fish.

If a thicker sauce is desired, mix 1 tablespoon cornstarch with 2 tablespoons cold water. Stir into strained stock and proceed as above. SERVES 6.

This is a good dish for a hot summer's day.

Baked Fish

Scale and clean a 2-pound whole fish. Insert 3 or 4 stalks of thyme or tarragon into cavity. Sprinkle the fish inside and out with salt and pepper, dredge it lightly with flour, and pour olive oil over it.

Bake at 400°F. in preheated oven until flesh flakes easily. Allow 12 to 15 minutes per pound of fish. Baste every 10 minutes. Add 1 tablespoon fresh lemon juice to liquid in pan a few minutes before removing fish from oven, and baste with the mixture. SERVES 4 OR 5.

Baked Whole Fish, Smyrna Style

2   pounds fish
3   tablespoons olive oil
½   teaspoon salt
¼   teaspoon pepper
3   tablespoons minced parsley
2   tablespoons minced onion
2   tablespoons butter
1   tablespoon lemon juice

Wash fish, drain thoroughly, roll in olive oil, and sprinkle with salt and pepper. Bake in oven preheated to 350°F. Blend together parsley, onion, butter, and lemon juice. When fish is tender, after about 15 minutes, cover with this mixture and brown under broiler. Serve hot with wedges of lemon. SERVES 4.

This dressing is sufficient for a 2-pound bluefish, mackerel, porgy, flounder, or red mullet. Neapolitans

add bread crumbs and minced garlic to the dressing and
spread it over the fish before baking.

Sliced Fish, Smyrna Style

> 2 tablespoons tomato sauce
> 2 tablespoons olive oil
> ¼ cup minced parsley
> 2 tablespoons lemon juice
>   Salt and pepper
> 1 pound sliced fish or fish steaks (halibut,
>   bass, porgy, or mackerel)

Bring tomato sauce and olive oil to boil with 1 cup water.
After 5 minutes add parsley and lemon juice. Cook till
blended, about 5 minutes longer, and pour the mixture
over the fish in shallow pan and let simmer 15 to 35
minutes, according to thickness of fish, or bake in a
slow oven in covered pan or casserole for 15 to 35
minutes. Brown fish lightly under broiler before serving.
SERVES 3 OR 4.

Fried Fish, Greek Style

Wash 1 pound of sliced fish, drain, sprinkle with salt.
Dip in flour to which pepper has been added.

Heat olive oil in skillet about ½ inch deep, until it
browns a cube of bread in 40 seconds. Add the fish and
brown gradually on each side. Transfer to platter.

To the olive oil in the pan add 1½ tablespoons of
wine vinegar, stirring well. Pour a small amount of the

mixture over each slice of fish. Serve warm with Mock Hollandaise Sauce. SERVES 3.

A simple but subtle variation on ordinary fried fish. When frying *fish steaks*, such as cod, halibut or salmon, dip in flour and beaten egg before frying.

Baked Fish with Mushrooms

(Mullet, whitefish, and weakfish are suggested)

2½ pounds boned fish
¼ cup olive oil
½ cup halved mushroom caps
1 carrot, diced
2 tablespoons chopped leek or onion
1 cup white wine
½ cup water or fish stock
   Salt and pepper to taste

Grease a baking pan with olive oil or butter. Wash fish thoroughly, drain, dry, and place in greased pan. Heat the olive oil in a 6-inch pan or skillet and sauté the mushrooms, carrot, and leek for 5 minutes. Add wine, water, and seasoning. Let simmer till the vegetables are tender but still firm.

Remove the vegetables, retaining liquid, and place vegetables on fish. Cover pan with aluminum foil or lid and bake in moderate oven (350°F.) for 15 to 20 minutes.

Reduce the liquid by half by boiling briskly, and pour over fish just before serving. SERVES 6.

Lemon and Olive Oil Sauce

Olive oil and lemon juice may be poured over fish at the table according to taste. Or beat thoroughly with fork in small bowl 2 parts of olive oil to 1 part of lemon juice, and pour over poached fish cooled to room temperature.

Mock Hollandaise à la Smyrna
[*Agristada*]

SMYRNA

2 eggs
1 teaspoon salt
Juice of 1 lemon
1 tablespoon flour

Break the eggs into a small (3-cup) saucepan and beat lightly with a fork. Add 1 tablespoon water, the salt, and the lemon juice. In a bowl make a paste of the flour and 2 tablespoons water.

Gradually stir paste into egg mixture. Cook this over low heat until it is the consistency of pudding. Pour into a bowl, and, when it has cooled slightly, put it in the refrigerator to chill. Serve sauce with fried fish. SERVES 4.

It is the custom to pour some of the olive oil in which fish has been fried over the dressing in the form of a simple circular design or letter. This imparts additional flavor and interest to the dish.

Mustard Sauce

Melt 3 tablespoons butter and stir in 1 tablespoon prepared mustard and 1 teaspoon boiling water. Serve warm with poached fish.

Prepared mustard: Mix together 2 tablespoons white wine vinegar, 2 tablespoons dry mustard, ¼ teaspoon sugar, pinch of salt, and 1 tablespoon olive oil.

Parsley and Onion Sauce

    2 tablespoons minced onion
    4 tablespoons coarsely cut Italian parsley
    ¼ teaspoon salt
    2 tablespoons lemon juice
    5 tablespoons olive oil

Mix together first 3 ingredients and add lemon juice and olive oil which have been thoroughly blended. Let stand for five minutes. Serve with poached or fried fish.

Tartar Sauce

    ½ cup mayonnaise
    2 teaspoons chopped capers
    1 tablespoon minced cucumber
    2 teaspoons tarragon vinegar
    2 teaspoons onion juice
       Minced onion or chives

Mix all ingredients. Serve with poached or fried fish.

Meats

Boiled Beef with Parsley and Lemon Sauce [*Carne Ervida*]

SMYRNA

- 1 pound chuck steak or 2 pounds flank
- 1 teaspoon salt
- 1 onion, cut in half

Cover meat with boiling water; add salt and onion. Cook over medium heat 40 to 60 minutes till tender. Serve with Parsley and Lemon Sauce. SERVES 4.

PARSLEY AND LEMON SAUCE

This sauce is used to garnish boiled beef; with rice on the side it is considered a complete entree.

- 1 tablespoon flour
  Juice of ½ lemon
- ½ cup chopped celery leaves
- ½ cup chopped parsley leaves
  Pinch of salt

Mix together flour, lemon juice, and enough water to make a loose paste. In a small saucepan cover the leaves with water. Bring to a boil. Add salt and stir in the paste. Let simmer on a very low heat 8 to 10 minutes. When ready to serve add a little water and reheat.

Casserole of Eggplant and Beef
[*Mousaka Melitzanes*]

GREECE

    1   pound eggplant
    2   tablespoons olive oil
    ½   pound chopped beef
    2   eggs
    1   tablespoon cracker crumbs
  1½   teaspoons salt
        Pepper

Peel eggplant and cut into slices about ¼ inch thick, in order to have enough for 3 layers. Boil in 1 quart salted water for 5 minutes. Drain thoroughly. Warm olive oil in a 1½-quart casserole. Do not scorch.

Place layer of eggplant in the heated olive oil. Mix chopped beef with 1 well-beaten egg, ¼ teaspoon salt, and pepper. Cover the eggplant with half of this mixture. Repeat layers of eggplant and meat mixture. Over top place a third layer of eggplant. Mix 1 egg with 1 tablespoon cracker crumbs and ¼ teaspoon salt. Spread over eggplant. Place in oven preheated to 350°F. for 15 minutes. Serve hot. SERVES 4.

NOTE: Two tablespoons grated cheese, preferably Romano, may be used instead of the cracker crumbs.

This makes a good lunch dish.

Beef Kebab

    2 pounds chuck steak 1 to 1½ inches thick
    3 ripe tomatoes, cut in quarters, or 1 can (1
           pound) tomatoes, drained
    2 onions, sliced
    2 green peppers, seeded and cut in strips
    1 tablespoon olive oil or suet
       Salt and pepper

Sear beef in a heavy skillet. In a Dutch oven or casserole,
arrange half the tomatoes, onions, and green peppers,
then the meat and olive oil, salt and pepper. Place remainder of vegetables over meat. Cover tightly and let
cook over low heat approximately 1 hour, or till tender.
SERVES 6.

Kebab Smyrna

    ⅓ cup olive oil
    1 cup tomato sauce
    1 teaspoon salt
    ¼ teaspoon pepper
    2 pounds chuck steak, about 2 inches thick

Place all ingredients except meat in a skillet or shallow
10-inch casserole. Add 1½ cups water. Bring to a boil
and let simmer till well blended. Cut meat into 3-inch
squares. Add to sauce and cook on low heat for about
1½ hours or till tender. Remove meat, and reduce liquid
on high heat till it is the texture of gravy. Replace meat
to heat. SERVES 6.

Meat Balls and Parsley à la Smyrna
[*Kopétas*]

    1 pound chopped chuck or neck meat
    ¾ teaspoon salt
    ¼ teaspoon pepper
    ½ cup minced Italian parsley
    2 tablespoons minced onion
    3 tablespoons olive oil
    3 tablespoons tomato sauce
    1 medium-sized potato, parboiled and
        quartered

Mix meat with salt, pepper, parsley, onion, and 1 tablespoon olive oil, either with fingers or stirring with a fork
to keep mixture light. Roll into balls no larger than 1½
to 2 inches in diameter. Bring 1 cup water, tomato
sauce, and 2 tablespoons olive oil to boil in a casserole.
Add meatballs and simmer for 15 minutes. Then add the
potato. Let simmer additional 15 minutes. SERVES 6.

Beef Patties with Celery Leaves
[*Keftez de Apio*]

SMYRNA

    1 small potato
    ⅓ cup coarsely cut celery leaves or celery and
        parsley leaves
    ¾ pound chopped beef

2 large eggs
¾ teaspoon salt
  Pepper to taste
2 tablespoons cracker crumbs
½ cup olive oil
½ cup tomato sauce
  Pinch of sugar
3 tablespoons lemon juice

Peel and cut potato in ¼-inch slices and cook rapidly in boiling salted water to cover. If celery leaves are coarse, cook briskly in water for 3 minutes. Drain.

In a bowl, mix lightly beef, 1 egg, celery leaves, ½ teaspoon salt, pepper, and 2 slices (about ¼ cup) potato, coarsely mashed. The mixture must be soft. Form into patties 2 inches across and ¾ inch thick, handling lightly. Do not pack. Have two dishes prepared, one with cracker crumbs, the second with 1 egg beaten with ¼ teaspoon of salt. Dip patties into cracker crumbs and egg. Set aside on plate. In 6-inch skillet heat olive oil ½ inch deep. Brown patties on both sides and place in metal casserole as they are finished. When all are browned add ½ of olive oil in which they were fried, tomato sauce, ¼ teaspoon salt, sugar and ½ cup water.

Bring to a boil, add lemon juice and reduce heat. Cover. Let simmer for ½ hour. Gravy will be formed. Serve hot. SERVES 4.

Beef Dolma

Stuffed vegetables are called *dolma* in and around Turkey. They are prepared with freshly ground meat, Italian parsley, and a fine olive oil. The flavor is unique and always evokes enthusiastic comment. The following two recipes are typical dolma dishes.

Stuffed Cabbage, Smyrna Style
[Lahano Dolmasi]

8 large cabbage leaves
1 pound lean chopped beef
½ cup minced Italian parsley
2 tablespoons minced onion
2 tablespoons white rice
¾ teaspoon salt
  Pepper to taste
4 tablespoons olive oil
3 tablespoons tomato sauce
1 tablespoon lemon juice

Peel off large outer leaves from cabbage, discarding the very coarse leaves. If leaves tear they still may be used. Soak in hot water to soften, about 5 minutes.

Meanwhile, in a bowl mix beef, parsley, onion, rice, salt, pepper, and 2 tablespoons olive oil, using fingers or a fork. Add 1 tablespoon cold water. Handle lightly and as little as possible.

In center of a large leaf, or of 2 smaller leaves overlapping, place a heaping tablespoon of the meat mixture. Fold over leaves. Place in casserole, pressing down firmly. Any extra leaves may be cut in small pieces and put between the dolma.

Pour over tomato sauce and water to half the depth,

the rest of the olive oil, pinch of salt, pepper, and lemon juice. Cook over low heat 30 to 40 minutes. Serve hot. SERVES 4 TO 6.

Stuffed Zucchini
[Kolokythia Yemista]

    2 pounds zucchini 1½ inches in diameter
    ¾ pound chopped beef
    1 tablespoon rice
    ¾ cup coarsely cut Italian parsley leaves
       Salt
       Freshly ground pepper
    3 or 4 tablespoons olive oil
    3 tablespoons tomato sauce

Scrape off the peel and cut zucchini into sections about 2 to 3 inches long. Scoop out center, leaving the wall and base ¼ inch thick. If pulp is tender, use as is; if tough sprinkle salt on it, add 1 tablespoon of water and let simmer to extract the juice.

In a bowl lightly mix meat, rice, parsley, seasoning to taste, and 1 tablespoon olive oil.

Fill zucchini sections lightly and lay them in casserole. Pour over tomato sauce and remaining olive oil and fill in with the pulp or juice of pulp. Sprinkle with ½ teaspoon salt and pepper, cover, and let simmer 20 to 30 minutes until walls of squash are tender but not mushy. Brown lightly under broiler.

Serve hot. When made in advance of meal, reheat in 350°F. oven. SERVES 4.

Stuffed Tomatoes
[*Tomates Yemistes*]

    6 medium-sized tomatoes (about 3 inches in
          diameter)
    ¾ pound lean chopped beef
    ½ cup coarsely cut parsley
    2 tablespoons minced onion
    2 tablespoons white rice, washed
    4 tablespoons olive oil
    ¾ teaspoon salt
       Pepper to taste
    2 tablespoons tomato sauce

Wash tomatoes, cut off tops, and scoop out pulp, leaving
a wall ¼ inch thick. Place pulp, except for 2 tablespoons,
in shallow casserole or skillet where the filled tomatoes
will be set. In a bowl mix the meat with parsley, onion,
rice, 1 tablespoon cold water, 1 tablespoon olive oil, and
2 tablespoons of the pulp, lightly and with as little handling as possible. Fill the tomatoes with this mixture.
Set in casserole or skillet, add salt, pepper, the rest of the
olive oil, and the tomato sauce. Cover and let simmer on
low heat for 45 minutes. SERVES 4.

Stuffed Green Peppers

Wash 6 peppers, cut off tops and remove seeds. Stuff
peppers with same filling used for Stuffed Tomatoes,
above. Proceed as for Stuffed Tomatoes. SERVES 4.

Tomatoes Stuffed and Fried
[*Tomate Rellenado*]

4 tomatoes
¾ pound chopped meat
1 egg, beaten
½ teaspoon salt
   Pepper
2 tablespoons cracker crumbs
½ cup olive oil
1 tablespoon tomato sauce
2 tablespoons tomato pulp

Cut tomatoes in half crosswise and scoop out, retaining pulp. Mix meat, one-half the beaten egg, and seasoning with fork. Fill tomatoes. Turn the tomatoes upside down, dip in cracker crumbs and egg. Brown lightly on both sides in hot olive oil. Then place in shallow pan with tomato sauce, tomato pulp, ½ cup water, and the olive oil in which they were browned. Cover and simmer till water is absorbed, about 20 minutes. Serve hot. SERVES 4.

Shoulder Lamb Chops, Smyrna Style

1 medium-sized onion, sliced, or 1 clove garlic, minced
2 tablespoons olive oil
1 cup stock or water
2 tablespoons tomato sauce
   Salt and pepper
4 shoulder lamb chops, 1 inch thick

Lightly brown onion or garlic in olive oil. Cool the olive oil and add liquid and seasoning. Cook till blended, about 10 minutes. Add chops from which all fat has been cut. Bring to boil, cover, lower heat, and let simmer for 40 minutes or until just tender. If there is too much fat from the meat, drain off. Serve hot. SERVES 4.

NOTE: A half inch of Italian or Hungarian dried mushroom enhances the flavor—noticeably. If other types of mushrooms are used, a whole dried mushroom will be required.

Grilled Lamb Chops, Turkish Style

    2 pounds shoulder lamb chops
    1 tablespoon olive oil
    1 clove garlic (optional)
    1 tablespoon dry white wine
    1 teaspoon thyme
    1 tablespoon grated onion
    ½ teaspoon salt

Trim off all the fat from the chops, wipe meat with damp cloth, and pound until ⅜ inch thick. Blend the rest of the ingredients and place the chops in the mixture. Put aside in a cool place for 2 hours. Turn meat over at the end of 1 hour. Drain and place under broiler until brown, turning once. Serve immediately. SERVES 4.

Turkish Casserole of Lamb

    2 pounds shoulder of lamb
    4 tablespoons olive oil

Salt and pepper
3 large potatoes, in thick slices
3 tomatoes, peeled and diced
6 to 9 scallions, chopped
1 pimiento, chopped
1 teaspoon chopped sorrel (optional)
3 cloves of garlic (optional)
½ cup red wine
6 lettuce leaves, shredded
4 tablespoons chopped dill

Wipe off meat, cut into 3-inch pieces, put in an earthenware or other type of heatproof casserole with olive oil, salt, and pepper. Cover tightly and cook for ½ hour in moderate oven preheated to 350°F. Add remaining ingredients, reserving the shredded lettuce and dill, and cook 1½ to 2½ hours longer. Add the lettuce and dill 15 minutes before serving and remove the garlic just before serving. SERVES 4.

In Turkey this dish is garnished with nasturtium flowers.

Herbed Lamb

Leg or rack of lamb
½ cup olive oil
1 clove garlic, mashed
1 scant teaspoon salt
¼ teaspoon pepper
½ teaspoon oregano

If using the rack of lamb, have butcher slash the roast every 2 chops, to facilitate serving. The flesh of young lamb should be definitely pink in tone. It is important to have lean meat for this dish.

Rub meat with a paste made of the olive oil, garlic, and seasoning. Let stand at room temperature for 2 hours. Place on a rack in roasting pan in oven preheated to 350°F. Roast, allowing approximately 25 minutes to a pound. Serve hot. SERVES 6.

Betty Eliopolous, Smyrna

Lamb Kebab

2½ to 3 pounds of neck of lamb, cut into
          chunks
  2 to 3 tablespoons olive oil
      Salt and pepper
¼ teaspoon oregano

Wipe off lamb. Brown meat slowly in olive oil on all sides in heavy skillet. Add seasoning. Cover and continue to cook on low heat for 45 minutes or until tender but not stringy.

If desired, potatoes may be added 20 minutes before serving. SERVES 6.

Lamb Stew with Baby Okra
[*Arni Me Bamies*]

½ pound fresh or frozen okra
2 teaspoons tomato paste
1 pound lamb, cut up as for stewing

¼ cup olive oil
1 medium-sized onion, sliced
  Salt and pepper
1 teaspoon lemon juice

Wash the okra and trim stems, being careful not to cut so close that seeds are exposed. Plunge in hot water for 5 minutes. Drain, add to tomato paste and 1½ cups water, which have been brought to a boil. Cook on low heat.

Brown the meat in hot olive oil, then the onion. Add the okra and tomato sauce. Salt and pepper to taste. Add lemon juice. Simmer for 30 to 40 minutes till meat is tender. Serve hot. SERVES 4.

Shish Kebab

Use leg of lamb boned and sliced 1 inch thick, or use shoulder of lamb. Place in a large earthen or glass bowl. Cover with hot water and wine vinegar (⅓ wine vinegar, ⅔ water) which have been boiled together. Let stand from 2 to 10 hours. Young lamb requires the minimum time.

Drain thoroughly in colander. Cut into pieces about 1½ inches square and marinate in the sauce (below) 1 to 2 hours. If the meat is properly dried the maximum flavor of the sauce is obtained.

Put the meat on skewers, alternating with halves of small onions and pieces of green pepper. Broil over charcoal embers 5 minutes on each side.

SAUCE FOR SHISH KEBAB

1 teaspoon caraway seeds (optional)
1 teaspoon oregano
½ teaspoon salt
  Pepper
¾ cup olive oil
1 clove garlic, minced (optional)
2 tablespoons onion juice

Crush caraway seeds with wooden mallet in brown paper. Mash together with oregano, salt, and pepper in a small bowl. Add olive oil, minced garlic, and onion juice.

This quantity of sauce is sufficient for 5 pounds of meat. Any leftover may be used to marinate tomatoes to be grilled or broiled on a skewer.

Mutton Casserole

3 pounds leg of mutton, boned and sliced
6 tablespoons olive oil
3 cups stock prepared from mutton bone
2 carrots, sliced
15 small white onions
2 large tomatoes, peeled
2 pimientos, sliced
1 cup green peas, fresh or canned
1 clove of garlic (optional)
3 tablespoons chopped dill

Wipe the meat off and cut into 2-inch squares. Heat the

olive oil and add the meat. Cook over low heat for ½ hour. Cover with boiling stock. Add the carrots. When they are parboiled, add the rest of the ingredients, except the dill. When the meat is tender sprinkle in the dill and serve immediately. SERVES 6.

Veal and Mushrooms

6 slices rump of veal or chops ¼ inch thick
  Flour
  Salt and pepper
⅓ cup olive oil
½ cup light meat stock or water
½ pound fresh mushrooms or 4-ounce can mushroom caps
5 tablespoons dry wine

Wipe off meat. Dredge with flour seasoned with salt and pepper.

Heat olive oil in a skillet gradually until it browns a cube of white bread. Add the chops and let brown slowly on each side. Add meat stock or water. Cover and cook on low heat ½ hour or till tender. When halfway through, add fresh mushrooms which have been cooked in salted water for 10 minutes, or drained canned mushroom caps. Stir wine into sauce. (Bardolino wine is suggested.) Let simmer for 5 minutes. Serve hot. SERVES 4.

Blanquette of Veal à la Tunis
[*Blanquette de Veau*]

    2 pounds veal, sliced thin and cut into 3-inch
           squares
   ½ cup olive oil
    1 medium-sized onion, sliced
    2 tablespoons flour
   ¾ teaspoon salt
   ¼ teaspoon pepper
    2 egg yolks
    4 tablespoons lemon juice

In a 9-inch skillet or shallow casserole braise the veal, using ¼ cup olive oil. Remove the meat and sauté the onion in the same oil till limp. Place the remainder of the olive oil in a small skillet and lightly sauté the flour, seasoned with a pinch of salt and pepper. Blend with the onion in the larger pan.

Replace the veal and cover with 1½ to 2 cups hot water or stock. Cover and let simmer till tender, about ½ hour, on very low heat. If necessary add two or three more tablespoons of water or stock to prevent sticking.

Just before serving, prepare sauce. Keep the meat warm while preparing the sauce. Beat the egg yolks thoroughly, adding the lemon juice. Stir in a little of the gravy drained from the meat. Then drain and stir in the rest of the gravy, using ¾ cup gravy per egg yolk. Spread some of the sauce over the meat in the platter and serve the rest from a gravy boat. SERVES 4.

Casserole of Veal
[*Dana Tas Etli Kebabi*]

TURKEY

2 pounds boned leg of veal, sliced
2 tablespoons chopped onion
1 teaspoon salt
½ teaspoon pepper
2 tablespoons fresh coconut, or canned flaked
    coconut
¼ teaspoon thyme
¼ teaspoon ground cloves
¼ cup chicken fat or
    olive oil
2 tomatoes, peeled
1 cup dry white wine

Wipe off the meat and cut into thick chunks—about 2 inches square. Place in a shallow casserole or skillet with the onion, salt, pepper, coconut, thyme, and cloves. Mix thoroughly and put aside in a cool place for 2 hours.

Heat the fat or olive oil and add it to the meat in the casserole. Sauté for 3 minutes, moving the pan continuously. Add the tomatoes and wine. Cover tightly. Cook over low heat 3 to 4 hours till meat is tender.

Serve hot with white or saffron rice. SERVES 6.

Veal, North Italian Style [*Vitello all'uccelletto: "Veal for the Little Bird"*]

1½ pounds top-quality veal, thinly sliced
5 tablespoons olive oil
1 teaspoon salt
  Pepper
3 tablespoons lemon juice
3 tablespoons white wine (optional)

Wipe off meat. Sear in hot but not burning olive oil. When seared add salt, pepper, and lemon juice. Stir in wine. Transfer to warm serving dish, sprinkle with parsley and serve hot. SERVES 4.

Veal Chops Milanese

4 veal chops, scant ½ inch thick
½ teaspoon salt
½ teaspoon pepper
1 egg, well beaten
1 cup bread crumbs
4 tablespoons olive oil
1 lemon, cut into wedges

Sprinkle the chops with salt and pepper. Dip them into the beaten egg and into the bread crumbs. Heat the olive oil in a frying pan, add chops, and fry slowly 10 minutes on each side. Veal must cook slowly and thoroughly. Transfer to warm platter and serve hot with the lemon wedges. SERVES 4.

Beef Liver in Vinegar Sauce

  1 pound liver, thickly sliced (⅜ inch)
  1 clove of garlic, cut in slivers
  ½ teaspoon salt
     Pepper (optional)
  2 tablespoons tomato sauce
  2 tablespoons olive oil
  2 tablespoons vinegar
1 ½ tablespoons flour

Sear liver under broiler on both sides till lightly browned.
Cut in one-inch squares. Put liver, garlic, salt, and pepper
in shallow casserole or skillet over low heat. Add tomato
sauce and olive oil and cover with water. Bring to a boil
and simmer. In a bowl mix vinegar, flour, and 2 tablespoons water till the consistency of soft custard. Pour
vinegar sauce in center of pan, stirring about three minutes till smooth and distributed.

Simmer entire mixture additional 5 minutes, being
sure that liver is tender but not overcooked. Serve hot.
SERVES 4 TO 6.

Calf's Liver with Onions

  1 pound calf's liver, cut in ½-inch slices
  3 tablespoons flour
  3 tablespoons olive oil
  1 large onion, sliced
     Salt and pepper to taste

Wash and drain liver. Remove skin from around the edge. Dredge the liver with flour. Heat the olive oil in a heavy skillet. Brown the onion, remove, and set aside in a pan where it can be reheated. Add the liver to the hot olive oil and sauté on medium heat till brown on each side (three minutes on each side for medium rare). Season and serve immediately on warm platter with the hot onions. SERVES 4.

Calf's Brains

Dismiss any prejudice you may have. Fresh calf's brains properly prepared have a most agreeable texture and flavor.

Preparation: Remove brains from refrigerator, let stand at room temperature for 20 minutes. Immerse in cold water and remove the membrane. Then proceed with either of the following recipes.

Fried Calf's Brains

    1 pair calf's brains
    1 tablespoon cider vinegar or lemon juice
    ⅓ cup flour slightly salted
    1 egg, beaten
    ⅓ cup olive oil

Place prepared brains (see above) in boiling salted water to cover, with 1 tablespoon cider vinegar or lemon juice. When the water comes to a boil again, remove brains and drain. Slice into patties about 2 inches in diameter and a scant half inch thick. Dip pieces in the flour and then in the beaten egg. In a small skillet fry 3 or 4 pieces at a time, in hot olive oil, till golden brown. Drain on brown paper. Serve hot with wedges of lemon or Olive Oil Mayonnaise. SERVES 3.

Calf's Brains in Tomato Sauce
SMYRNA

2 tablespoons tomato sauce
   Scant teaspoon salt
¼ teaspoon pepper
1 pair calf's brains sliced and fried (see Fried
      Calf's Brains recipe)
3 tablespoons olive oil in which brains were
      fried
1 tablespoon lemon juice

In a shallow pan or skillet bring 1 cup of water and tomato sauce to a boil. Add the seasoning, the previously fried patties, the olive oil and the lemon juice. Simmer for 10 minutes, or until the liquid is the consistency of gravy. Serve hot. SERVES 3 OR 4.

Poultry

Boiled Chicken

Dress, clean, and cut a 5-pound fowl in pieces, or leave whole. Rub with salt. Place in deep pot and cover with boiling water. Let simmer 3 hours or until tender. One-half hour before serving add 1 carrot, a stalk of celery cut into 2-inch pieces, and a medium-sized onion. SERVES 4 TO 6.

Browned Stewed Chicken

Cook chicken whole as above. When tender, roll chicken in olive oil or chicken fat. Brown chicken in hot oven (475°F.) for 15 to 25 minutes; baste with 1 cup of the stock in which it was boiled. When browned, cover to retain juices, and keep warm at reduced heat till ready to serve. SERVES 4 TO 6.

Stewed chicken may also be embellished by serving with sauce of Chicken Andaluz, below.

Chicken Andaluz [*Coria del Rio*]

ANDALUCÍA, SPAIN

1 5-pound chicken
1 clove garlic
4 tablespoons olive oil
1 medium onion, sliced
3 tablespoons blanched almonds
Salt and pepper
2 tablespoons minced parsley
¾ cup dry sherry

Cut chicken into 8 pieces, rub with salt, cover with water, and stew until tender. Fry clove of garlic in hot olive oil and discard garlic. In same oil, fry sliced onion till limp and blanched almonds till lightly browned. Crush the almonds and mash them with the onion. Add salt and pepper, parsley and sherry, blending all together thoroughly. Heat slightly, beat, and pour over hot chicken, arranged on a platter, and serve. SERVES 6 TO 8.

Roast Chicken

First Method. (*In an uncovered roasting pan*): Dress and clean chicken. Rub outside with a cut clove of garlic. Rub cavity with salt. Brush with olive oil or poultry fat. Season with salt and pepper. Four stems of tarragon or oregano (free of the leaves) placed in the cavity will enhance the flavor. Place chicken on its side on rack in uncovered pan in hot oven (475°F.). When it is lightly browned turn it. When brown on both sides reduce heat to 300°F., and turn chicken onto its back for remainder of roasting time. Or roast at 325°F. for the entire period with chicken on its back for whole time.

Brush or baste with fat from the pan every 20 minutes. Roast 20 minutes to the pound.

Second Method. (In a covered roasting pan): Prepare as above. Place chicken on its back on the rack in pan. Pour 1 cup of water or stock made from the giblets into pan below the rack. Cover, and, with vent open, roast at 450°F. until brown. Then close vent and reduce heat to 325°F. Or keep vent closed and roast for entire period at 375°F.

Roast Chicken, Spanish Style

(Simplified)

    1   4½ to 5-pound roasting chicken
        Salt and pepper
    1   clove garlic
    4   tablespoons olive oil
    ½   teaspoon oregano
    1   medium onion, sliced
    1   cup Italian tomatoes, cut small
    2   medium-sized green peppers, cut up
    ¾   pound small mushrooms (washed and
            drained)

Dress and clean chicken. Season inside and out with salt and pepper. Rub outside with a cut clove of garlic. Roll in olive oil to which oregano has been added.

Roast in open pan in hot oven (450°F.). When browned, reduce heat to 375°F., add onion and tomatoes. Cover and continue roasting 1 to 1¼ hours, or till tender.

Twenty minutes before chicken is finished, add the green peppers and mushrooms. SERVES 6.

Chicken with Mushrooms

  1 3½-pound young chicken
  ¼ cup olive oil
  1 small onion, sliced
     Salt
     Freshly ground pepper
  1 pound fresh mushrooms

Dress and clean chicken, leaving whole or cutting at joints. Heat olive oil in deep frying pan or casserole. Brown chicken. Add onion, salt, and pepper. Cover tightly and let simmer for an hour or until tender. Wash mushrooms and cook 5 minutes in boiling salted water. Drain and add to chicken. Cook for additional 15 minutes. Serve hot. SERVES 4.

Blanquette of Chicken
[*Blanquette de Poulet*]

On a sunny spring day in Tunis we were entertained for lunch in the large, gay dining room in the home of Monsieur Guez. The fare was so delicious and so appropriate for the time of day that we requested the recipe, which our host's international chef wrote out for us proudly and joyfully. This version is simpler than usual, but it is nevertheless subtle and flavorsome.

        1 3-pound chicken cut into small portions
        ½ cup olive oil
        1 medium-sized onion, diced
        2 tablespoons flour
        ¾ teaspoon salt
        ¼ teaspoon pepper
           Juice of 1 lemon
        2 egg yolks

Using a 9-inch shallow casserole or skillet, braise the chicken in one-half the olive oil. Remove, and sauté the onion in same casserole till limp. In a small skillet sauté the flour, salt, and pepper in the rest of the olive oil. Blend with the onion in the casserole. Replace the chicken, cover with hot water or stock prepared from giblets and simmer on low heat till tender, about ½ hour.

When chicken is ready to be served, prepare sauce. Keep the chicken warm while preparing the sauce. Beat the egg yolks with the lemon juice thoroughly. Stir in a little of the gravy drained from the chicken. Then drain and stir in the rest of the gravy, using ¾ cup of gravy to each egg yolk. When serving, pour some of the sauce over the chicken and serve the remainder in a gravy boat. SERVES 4.

Chicken with Rice [*Arroz con Pollo*]

    3 3-pound chickens, cut into 6 pieces each
       Salt
    3 cups olive oil
    2 cloves garlic
    2 green peppers, seeded and cut into 1-inch
          strips
    1 large (32-ounce) can Italian plum tomatoes
    2 8-ounce cans tomato sauce
    ½ teaspoon sugar
       Salt and pepper
    1 small can pimientos
    3 cups stock from giblets
    ⅛ teaspoon saffron
    1 large (1-pound) can petits pois (small
          peas)
    3 cups uncooked rice

Utensils needed:
      3-quart saucepan for preparing stock
      10-inch skillet or small roasting pan
      2-quart pot for sauce
      12-inch pottery casserole

Wash the chicken thoroughly, drain, and salt. Prepare stock from giblets and wings.

In a large skillet heat 2 cups of olive oil and brown 1 clove garlic and the green peppers. Discard the garlic and set aside the green peppers. Brown the chicken lightly, then drain off the olive oil and set aside while preparing the sauce and the rice.

In a saucepan (2-quart) prepare the sauce, putting in the canned tomatoes, tomato sauce, sugar, ½ cup of the olive oil in which the chickens were sautéed, salt and pepper to taste, minced garlic (the second clove), the sautéed green peppers, 2 tablespoons uncooked olive oil, and 2 cups water. Let simmer over low heat until well blended, about 2 hours.

Wash rice in a bowl of cold, salted water carefully so as not to nick the kernels. Rinse in tepid water. Bring stock to a boil, add olive oil (hot enough to brown a small piece of bread), salt, saffron, and lastly the rice. Let mixture come to a boil, uncovered. After 5 minutes, cover, reduce heat and let it cook additional 25 minutes. When kernels are tender but firm and the liquid absorbed, remove lid, turn off heat, and allow steam to escape. Stir rice gently from sides and bottom of pan.

Add chicken to the well-blended sauce and let simmer until almost tender, about ½ hour. (The cooking process is completed in the casserole.)

In a 12-inch pottery casserole arrange a layer of the cooked rice 1 inch deep, then a layer of chicken and the sauce. Repeat layers. Cover with a layer of rice, topped with a layer of peas. Put in oven preheated to 375°F. one-half hour before serving, thus allowing time for the cooking of chicken to be completed. A few minutes before serving, garnish with ½-inch strips of pimiento. Serve piping hot. SERVES 8.

This dish is suitable for large dinner parties because it can be prepared well in advance.

Chicken with Olives
[*Pollo alle Olive*]

    1 3½-pound chicken, disjointed
    3 tablespoons olive oil
    1 carrot, minced
    1 small tomato, diced
    1 onion, minced
       Stock from giblets
   15 ripe olives
       Salt and pepper to taste
    3 tablespoons tomato sauce

Lightly brown the chicken in hot olive oil. Add the carrot, tomato, and finally the onion. When the onion is golden brown, cover with boiling stock. Add 4 olives cut up, the mashed pulp of 4 olives, and the remainder of the olives whole. Add salt and pepper sparingly since olives are already salty. Add tomato sauce and simmer slowly till tender, about ½ hour. SERVES 4.

Chicken Livers

Wash and drain liver. Dredge with flour. Fry in hot olive oil ¼ inch deep. Serve immediately on toast or with white rice.

Duck with the French Touch
[*Caneton à la Bigarde*]

Wash duck thoroughly and dry it. Season with salt and
pepper. Place on rack in a roasting pan in a very hot
oven (500°F.) for ½ hour. Reduce heat to 300°F. A
young fowl requires no water; water or stock made from
the giblets may be used to baste an older bird. Prick
the skin with a fork from time to time to let the fat out.
Roast 2 to 4 hours (20 minutes to the pound) till the
meat on breast and legs is tender. When duck is about
half done, pour the juice of 1 navel orange over it.

Skim most of fat from the pan. To make gravy add
2 tablespoons flour and 1 cup hot water.

If a navel orange is not available, add 1 teaspoon
lemon juice to the juice of a Florida orange.

Roast Turkey [*Pavo Asado*]

Dress, clean, and season the bird. Stuff and tie down the
legs and wings. Sew up cavity with heavy white thread.
With ½ cup of olive oil brush the surface of the turkey.
Place it on its side on a rack in an uncovered roasting pan
in a hot oven (450°F.). Brown on one side for 5 minutes, turn and brown on the other side additional 5 minutes. Reduce heat to 325°F. and continue to roast at
325°F. for the entire time. Baste every 15 minutes.

Roast 15 to 30 minutes per pound according to age
and size of the bird. When the breast meat is tender the
turkey is done.

Stuffing for Poultry

    1 pound Italian chestnuts, baked or blanched and
        cut in half
    4 cups stale mixed white and rye bread, cut
        into pieces
    ¼ cup olive oil
    1 large onion, diced
    1 egg
    1 teaspoon salt
      Pepper
    4 tablespoons coarsely cut Italian parsley
      Liver, gizzard and heart of bird, parboiled
        and diced
    1 teaspoon oregano

Prepare chestnuts by one of the methods below. Cut them in half. Soak bread in cold water and squeeze it dry. In a skillet heat olive oil and sauté onion till limp. Add the bread, the egg slightly beaten, seasoning, parsley, and the heart, liver, and tender parts of gizzard. Lastly, add the chestnuts and oregano. Makes enough stuffing for a 15-pound bird.

Blanched Chestnuts: Cover chestnuts with boiling water. Cook briskly for 15 to 20 minutes till shell and skin can be removed easily.

Baked Chestnuts: Make a ½-inch slit on the flat side of the chestnuts with a sharp knife. Place in a pan. Bake over moderate heat for 10 minutes, shaking pan from time to time. Remove shell and inner skin at the same time.

Salads and Salad Dressings

Cabbage Salad [*Cole Slaw*]

You cannot compare cole slaw prepared from young green cabbage with the product generally served in restaurants. Slaw prepared from the young cabbage garnished with a fine French dressing or an olive oil mayonnaise is a veritable repast! It is most popular in Greece and Turkey.

Cut young, green cabbage in quarters. Wash. Soak in cold, slightly salted water for about 5 minutes. Drain thoroughly. Shred cabbage in strips about ⅛ inch wide, thereby conserving maximum flavor. Sprinkle with salt and place in refrigerator. Blend well 1 tablespoon lemon juice with 2 tablespoons olive oil. When ready to serve salad, pour this dressing over it. When fresh Spanish onions are available they may be added, as well as rings of green pepper. If desired, add 1 tablespoon mayonnaise.

Greek Salad

      9 romaine or iceberg lettuce leaves
      2 tomatoes, diced
      1 onion or 3 scallions, diced
    ½ cucumber, diced
      3 tablespoons minced parsley
      6 to 8 ripe olives
      4 to 6 anchovies

Shred washed lettuce leaves, drain well, and mix with other ingredients. Serve with French Dressing. SERVES 4.

Mixed Green Salad

Chicory   Endive cut into
Escarole   1-inch pieces
Romaine lettuce Sliced green
Watercress   pepper
Avocado   French Dressing
                    (see page 73)

Any one or more of the above leafy ingredients combined with either the avocado, endive, or green pepper and French Dressing make a light salad of interesting texture.

It is important that the leaves be *thoroughly* dried after washing so that the salad dressing is not diluted. To retain the maximum flavor and vitamin value of the leaves, prepare only one day's supply. Wash, drain, dry, and chill leaves. Just before serving break into 2-inch

pieces. Place in a wooden bowl which has been rubbed
with garlic. Sprinkle the leaves lightly with salt. Pour
the French Dressing, which has been thoroughly beaten,
over the leaves.

Turkish Salad

9   romaine or iceberg lettuce leaves
2   tomatoes, diced
1   onion or 3 scallions, diced
½   cucumber, diced
3   tablespoons minced parsley
2   tablespoons wine vinegar
6   tablespoons olive oil
¼   teaspoon sugar
    Salt to taste

In a bowl shred the washed lettuce leaves and mix with
other vegetables. Blend the parsley with the liquid ingredients and seasoning, which have been thoroughly
beaten. Pour dressing over the vegetables. SERVES 4.

Roman-Style Mixed Salad

½   head of romaine lettuce
    Sliced heart of fennel
4   sliced radishes
1   tablespoon cooked peas (optional)
2   tomatoes, sliced
2   tablespoons olive oil
4   tablespoons lemon juice
    Salt and pepper

Place first 4 ingredients in a bowl. Chill. In a small bowl beat the olive oil, lemon juice, and seasoning. Add tomatoes to salad. Pour dressing over the salad, toss, and serve immediately. SERVES 4.

Mixed Spring Vegetable Salad

½ pound green beans
½ pound zucchini, sliced
1 large tomato or 3 plum tomatoes, halved
½ teaspoon salt
3 tablespoons olive oil
3 tablespoons lemon juice
Salt and pepper

Cook beans and zucchini separately in a minimum amount of water to which ¼ teaspoon salt has been added. Chill; add raw tomatoes. At the table add olive oil, lemon, and seasoning. SERVES 6.

Tomato Salads

In the summer and fall when tomatoes are abundant and sweet, they can be served in various combinations.

Caution! Do not add tomatoes to salads until the last minute; otherwise the juice will dilute the dressing.

Tomatoes and Small Yellow Peppers

In a bowl mix equal parts of quartered tomatoes with sliced yellow peppers. Season with salt and pepper. Pour over it a mixture of two parts olive oil to one part lemon juice or cider vinegar thoroughly blended.

Tomatoes, Green Peppers, and Onion

Follow directions in above recipe, mixing equal parts of quartered tomatoes, sliced peppers, and onions, being sure that the onions are young and sweet.

Tomatoes, Onion, and Parsley

        3 tomatoes, washed and cut into eighths
        1 medium onion, sliced
        ½ cucumber, sliced (optional)
        ⅓ cup chopped parsley
        2 tablespoons olive oil
        1 tablespoon lemon juice
           Salt
           Freshly ground pepper to taste

Place first four ingredients in a bowl or serving dish. In a small bowl beat thoroughly the olive oil, lemon juice, and seasoning. Pour dressing over the salad. Toss and serve at once. SERVES 6.

Tomatoes with Thyme or Oregano

Wash and cut tomatoes in half crosswise. For the dressing blend thoroughly two parts olive oil to one part lemon juice or vinegar, seasoning, ¼ teaspoon herbs, and a suspicion of garlic (about ⅛ teaspoon), if desired. If the tomatoes are not sufficiently ripe, they may be grilled with this dressing, and then lightly browned.

French Dressing

> ¼ teaspoon salt
> ⅛ teaspoon freshly ground pepper
> ⅛ teaspoon dry mustard
>   2 tablespoons wine vinegar or lemon juice
>   4 to 6 tablespoons fine olive oil
>   Capers, oregano, or Worcestershire
>   (optional)

In a small bowl blend dry ingredients. Add half the vinegar, then the olive oil and the rest of the vinegar. Beat thoroughly.

The dressing may be varied by using tarragon vinegar, or by adding capers, oregano, or a few drops of Worcestershire sauce.

Lemon and Olive Oil Dressing

This simplest of dressings consists of 3 parts of olive oil to 1 part of lemon juice, plus desired seasoning. It may be used on lettuce or any cooled cooked vegetable.

Olive Oil Mayonnaise

Mayonnaise prepared from a good olive oil has a noticeably more delicate flavor and texture than the dressing prepared from nondescript oils. It contributes to boiled chicken and poached fish a surprising nuance and interest.

    1 egg yolk or whole egg
    1 teaspoon salt
    ¼ teaspoon pepper
    ¼ teaspoon dry mustard
       Pinch of sugar
    1 cup olive oil
    1 tablespoon cider vinegar
    1 tablespoon lemon juice
    1 tablespoon freshly grated onion
    ¼ teaspoon minced garlic

Beat egg and mix in salt, pepper, mustard, and sugar. Add olive oil, ¼ teaspoon at a time, until 1 tablespoon is absorbed, beating only enough to blend. Then add olive oil more liberally, a tablespoon at a time. When mixture is the proper thick consistency, add vinegar, lemon juice and then onion and garlic. Properly refrigerated, mayonnaise prepared this way lasts three weeks.

If there is any interruption during the preparation, the mixture must be beaten before more olive oil is added. Should the mixture curdle through excessive beating, start again. Beat a fresh egg or egg yolk, adding the previous mixture gradually until it is the desired consistency. MAKES SLIGHTLY OVER 1 CUP.

Roquefort Cheese Dressing

    2 ounces Roquefort cheese
    2 tablespoons cream or olive oil
 1½ tablespoons lemon juice

Mash cheese thoroughly and add cream or olive oil. When a paste is formed, add the lemon juice. Serve with romaine lettuce or celery.

Vegetables

The following vegetables may be cooked in boiling salted water (1 teaspoon salt to a quart) and when cool may be served with freshly squeezed lemon and olive oil.

Prepared this way, they may be served as an appetizer or as a vegetable.

Asparagus
Broccoli
Cabbage
Dandelion Leaves
Cauliflower

String Beans
Wax Beans
Spinach
Escarole
Swiss Chard

Asparagus

Snap off lower tough ends of stalks, remove scales, and wash. Cook about 20 minutes in boiling salted water in lower half of double boiler (or in a tall pot such as a percolator).

The top of the double boiler may be inverted over asparagus, permitting the tips to be steamed. Serve cool with olive oil and lemon juice to taste.

Fava Beans [*Habas Frescas*]

SPAIN

Fava beans appear in the spring and are a welcome change after the limited choice of winter vegetables. Be sure to get the true fava bean and not the coarse, flavorless horse bean.

    2 pounds fava beans
    1 medium onion, sliced
    3 tablespoons olive oil
    ¼ teaspoon sugar
    2 ounces parboiled or leftover beef, cut into
            2-inch chunks (optional)
    1 teaspoon salt

Wash beans with pods. Remove beans from pods but retain those pods which are succulent and young, breaking them up into pieces 1½ inches long. Sauté the onion in olive oil till limp, and add the beans and usable cut pods. Then cover with 2½ to 3 cups water and add the sugar. Fifteen minutes later add the meat, if desired. When the beans are tender add the salt. Serve hot. SERVES 6.

Lima Beans with Tomato Sauce

    2 pounds lima beans
    1 medium-sized onion, sliced
    3 tablespoons olive oil

2 tablespoons tomato sauce
1 teaspoon salt

Shell and wash lima beans. Sauté the onion in hot olive oil till limp. Cool, and add 2 cups water and tomato sauce. Bring to a boil and add the lima beans and salt. Cook 20 minutes or till tender. A few chunks of boiled meat or chicken will add flavor. Serve hot. SERVES 4.

Wide Green Beans with Herbs

1 pound fresh wide green beans
1 tablespoon lemon juice
 Salt to taste
 Grape leaves
1 tablespoon chopped mint
1 tablespoon chopped dill
6 scallions, cut in 2-inch pieces
1 teaspoon sugar
¼ cup olive oil

Wash the beans and leave them whole. Pour the lemon juice over them. Sprinkle with salt and put aside for 15 minutes. Line the bottom of a wide saucepan with grape leaves and lay on these the largest beans. Pile the mint, dill, and scallions in the center. Cover with remainder of the beans. Sprinkle with sugar, add ¾ cup water and the olive oil. Cover tightly and cook 15 to 30 minutes until beans are tender but unbroken. Do not uncover during cooking but shake occasionally to prevent sticking.

Let cool in saucepan. Chill and serve with yoghurt. SERVES 6.

Green Beans with Tomato Sauce
[*Fasoulia*]

GREECE

    1 pound green beans
    1 cup meat stock or water
    2 tablespoons olive oil
    2 tablespoons tomato sauce or 2 teaspoons
          tomato paste
    1 teaspoon salt

Prepare the beans in the "French" way: wash the beans and slit them down the length, then in half crosswise. Bring stock, olive oil, and tomato sauce to a boil; add salt and beans. Cook briskly for 15 to 25 minutes. Serve with the sauce in which they are cooked. SERVES 6.

Sworn vegetable haters devour beans cooked in this way. Wax beans may be prepared in the same manner. The flavor is enhanced if you add a carrot or onion, and the neck or gizzard of a chicken while cooking. Moroccans add a clove of garlic to the stock.

Broccoli

Select broccoli with bright green closed flowerets. Break off coarse stalk. Soak in salted water for 10 minutes. Drain, place in boiling water and cook in open pot for 10 to 25 minutes, till tender but not soft, or cook same way as asparagus, steaming tips. Cool, and serve at room temperature with olive oil and lemon juice.

Cabbage in Tomato Sauce, Smyrna Style [*Col con Tomate*]

2 tablespoons olive oil
2 tablespoons tomato sauce
  Salt to taste
1 small cabbage (about 1 pound), cut in
    eighths
2 teaspoons lemon juice

In a saucepan put enough water to cover cabbage, add olive oil and tomato sauce. Bring to a boil. Add salt, cabbage, and lemon juice. Cook briskly till tender. Serve warm with the sauce in which it is cooked. SERVES 6.

Carrots and Mint

Scrape, wash, and dice carrots or slice them crosswise. Cook in boiling salted water until tender, 10 to 15 minutes. Drain. Stir in sweet butter to taste. Sprinkle with coarsely cut fresh mint leaves.

Boiled Cauliflower

Remove cauliflower leaves and cut off stalk. Soak the cauliflower with head down in cold, salted water for 5 minutes. Cook the cauliflower in rapidly boiling salted water in an open pot till tender, 15 to 30 minutes. Drain and cool. Serve with olive oil and lemon juice.

Fried Cauliflower

Prepare cauliflower and cook as directed above. When it is cool, cauliflower may be broken into individual flowerets, dipped in flour and fried till golden brown in olive oil in which a clove of garlic has been browned.

Cauliflower au Gratin

Put whole boiled cauliflower in buttered or oiled baking dish. Dot with butter. Sprinkle with bread crumbs and 2 tablespoons grated cheese, and brown lightly under broiler.

Celery and Almonds
[*Apio con Almendras*]

2 tablespoons almonds
4 tablespoons olive oil
   Salt to taste
3 cups celery (1 bunch, washed and cut into
    1½-inch lengths)
1 tablespoon lemon juice
1 large potato, quartered and parboiled

Blanch, drain almonds. When dry, brown in 2 tablespoons hot olive oil in small skillet.

Bring 1½ cups water and remaining olive oil to a

boil. Add salt, celery, and lemon juice, and simmer for
15 minutes. Then add the potato and almonds and cook
15 to 20 minutes longer. Serve hot. SERVES 6.

Celery and Chestnuts, Smyrna Style
[*Apio con Castañas*]

This dish is appropriate in the fall and winter when
chestnuts are available. Even the aroma of roasted chestnuts is a tonic. Fried almonds may be substituted when
chestnuts are not available, or chicken broth may be
used for part of the liquid.

    ½ pound Italian chestnuts
    4 tablespoons olive oil
       Salt to taste
    3 cups celery (1 bunch, washed and cut into
           1½-inch lengths)
    1 tablespoon lemon juice
    1 large potato, quartered and parboiled

Cut a cross into flat side of chestnuts; sprinkle with
water. Spread in flat pan and roast in hot oven for 20
minutes. While they are roasting, prepare liquid. To 1½
cups water and olive oil, which have been brought to a
boil, add salt, celery, and lemon juice. Then remove shells
from chestnuts, cut in half and add, together with potato, to above mixture. Simmer for about 20 minutes
longer. When celery is done, remove. Reduce liquid to
a light gravy texture. Serve hot. SERVES 8.

Celery Root
[Raiz de Apio]

    1 pound celery root
    2 tablespoons olive oil
       Scant teaspoon salt
       Pepper
    3 to 4 tablespoons lemon juice
    1 medium-sized potato, peeled and quartered
    ¼ teaspoon sugar

Wash and peel celery root and cut in cubes. Boil 2 cups
of water with the olive oil. Add salt, pepper, celery root,
lemon juice. Place potato on top and a pinch of sugar.

Cook till tender, adding water if necessary. When
the celery is tender the liquid should be a gravy texture.
SERVES 4 TO 6.

Chick Peas in Tomato Sauce
[Garbanzos en Tomate]

    2 tablespoons olive oil
    ½ cup tomato sauce
    ½ cup consomme
       Salt
       Pinch of sugar
    ½ pound dried chick peas, cooked; or canned
          chick peas from which brine has been
          drained

Heat the liquid ingredients and seasonings. Pour mixture

over the chick peas, which have been drained. Serve
warm. If desired, brown lightly under broiler. SERVES 3.

Chick Peas with Red or White Rice
[*Arroz con Garbanzos*]

SPAIN

Place prepared Red Rice (page 105) or Rice Pilaf (page
104) in casserole and stir in ½ cup canned or boiled
chick peas. Warm in slow oven. SERVES 6.

Dandelion Leaves

Snap off stalks, wash leaves, and drain in colander. Put
about ¼ inch of water in a saucepan, add leaves, and
cook on medium heat till tender, 5 to 8 minutes. Serve
cool with lemon and olive oil.

Chopped Eggplant
[*Melitzanes Salata*]

1 small or medium-sized eggplant
1 clove garlic, minced
1 to 2 tablespoons olive oil
   Salt and pepper to taste

Broil eggplant on a skewer directly over burner, rotating
until uniformly softened. Cut in half lengthwise and
scoop pulp from shell. Chop eggplant into a bowl, adding

minced garlic, enough olive oil to give a smooth pudding-like consistency, and the seasoning. Replace in shell and serve hot or serve cool with crackers or toast, garnished with parsley or sliced green pepper. SERVES 6.

Broiled Eggplant [*Berenjena*]

> 1 medium-sized eggplant
> 2 cloves garlic, minced
> 1 teaspoon grated onion
> ½ teaspoon salt
> ¼ cup olive oil

Cut eggplant in ½-inch slices and peel. Place the slices on a greased baking sheet. Mix together the garlic, onion, salt, and oil, and brush this onto the slices. Broil slices about five inches from the source of heat for 5 minutes, basting once with the seasoned olive oil. Turn slices, using a pancake turner, and brush with remaining olive oil mixture. Broil for about 2 minutes or until tender. Serve plain. SERVES 4.

Fried Eggplant

Peel and slice eggplant lengthwise about ½ inch thick. Soak in cold, salted water for about 5 to 10 minutes to extract bitterness. Drain.

Dip eggplant in flour and fry slices in hot olive oil until golden brown (oil is hot enough when it browns a small piece of bread). Serve hot.

Eggplant à la Smyrna I
[*Melitzanes Yachni*]

1 ¾-pound eggplant
1 medium-sized onion, sliced
4 tablespoons olive oil
½ cup tomato sauce
   Pinch of sugar
¾ teaspoon salt
   Pepper

Peel and slice eggplant lengthwise about ½ inch thick. Soak the eggplant in cold, salted water for 5 to 10 minutes to extract bitterness.

Braise in hot olive oil and transfer to saucepan or shallow casserole, draining off all but 1 tablespoon olive oil. Use more olive oil if necessary but be sure to leave only 1 tablespoon of oil after draining. Add ¼ cup water, onion, tomato sauce, and sugar. Season and simmer in covered pan until the eggplant is soft. Parboiled or leftover meat may be added 20 minutes after the ingredients are put in casserole. Continue to cook for 15 to 20 minutes. Serve hot. SERVES 4.

Eggplant à la Smyrna II

Prepare eggplant according to directions in the first paragraph of the above recipe. Place in shallow pan or casserole with ¼ cup water, sliced onion, salt, pinch of sugar, and 2 tablespoons olive oil. Stew slowly until eggplant is completely tender. Cook thoroughly, mashing from time to time. Serve hot.

Eggplant and Okra

    12 okra pods
     1 medium-sized eggplant, peeled and cubed
     1 onion, sliced
     3 tomatoes, cut in eighths
     1 tablespoon olive oil
        Salt and pepper
     1 tablespoon minced parsley

Wash okra, removing stem and tip. Cut across in ½-inch slices. Peel and slice eggplant lengthwise about ½ inch thick. Soak in cold, salted water for 5 to 10 minutes to extract bitterness. Place eggplant in a shallow pan or casserole with onion, tomatoes, okra, olive oil, salt, and pepper and simmer for ½ hour. Sprinkle with parsley and serve. SERVES 6.

Eggplant and Capers à la Naples

     1 2-pound eggplant
     1 onion, sliced
    ¼ cup olive oil
     1 clove garlic
    ½ cup tomato sauce
    ⅓ cup capers, drained
     1 teaspoon salt
        Pepper to taste

Peel and cut eggplant into 1½-inch cubes. Sauté onion in hot olive oil until limp. Add eggplant, garlic, tomato sauce, and capers. Cook additional 20 minutes. Remove garlic. Season and serve hot. SERVES 6.

Mrs. Velia Tosi, Roxbury, Mass.

Eggplant and Ricotta Cheese

    1 2-pound eggplant, cut in thin slices (scant
          ½ inch)
1½ cups canned plum tomatoes
    3 tablespoons olive oil
       Salt and pepper
 ½ pound ricotta or mozzarella cheese

Soak eggplant in salted water 5 minutes. Drain till dry.

Mix together tomatoes, olive oil, and 1 cup water in a saucepan and bring to a boil. Add seasoning to taste. Add eggplant and simmer on low heat for ½ hour. Turn mixture into a baking dish.

Place ricotta by teaspoonfuls on top of mixture or lay on mozzarella in thin slices. Put in oven preheated to 350°F. and bake 15 minutes. SERVES 6.

Suitable for a lunch dish.

Endive

    1 pound endive
 ¼ teaspoon salt
       Pinch of sugar
    2 teaspoons butter or 2 teaspoons olive oil
 ½ teaspoon lemon juice

Wash and drain endive. Cut in half lengthwise and place in saucepan. Cover with water and add salt, sugar, and butter or olive oil. Bring to a boil. Let cook briskly until tender and until water is evaporated. Add lemon juice and serve hot. SERVES 6.

This delicate vegetable dish enhanced our luncheon at the Voile au Vent Restaurant, Cannes.

Leeks [*Prasa con Tomate*]

Leek, although regarded as a soup green, is very flavorsome when prepared as a vegetable.

        1 bunch of leeks (about 2 pounds)
    1½ cups meat stock or water
        2 tablespoons tomato sauce
        2 tablespoons olive oil
           Salt and pepper
        2 tablespoons lemon juice
           Leftover boiled beef (optional)

Remove roots and outer layers of leeks. Wash leeks and cut in pieces 1½ inches long, using also those green parts of stalk which are succulent and not too stringy. Very wide stalks should be cut down the center. Place in hot water for about 5 minutes to draw out bitterness. Drain.

Combine and cook stock (beef or chicken) or water, tomato sauce, olive oil, salt, and pepper. When blended, add leeks and lemon juice. Cook 20 minutes or until tender. Transfer to casserole and brown lightly under broiler. A chunk or two of boiled beef added ten minutes before serving varies the flavor. SERVES 6.

This makes a very piquant dish. Small white onions or shallots may be cooked in the same way.

Leek Pie [*Fritada de Prasa*]

1 2-pound bunch of leeks
1 large boiled potato, mashed
4 eggs
¾ cup grated Romano cheese
  Salt
4 tablespoons olive oil

Prepare leek as in first paragraph of preceding recipe. Cook in salted water to cover until tender. Drain thoroughly (liquid may be used for soup).

Add mashed potato, eggs, cheese, and salt, stirring until mixture is uniform. Heat olive oil slightly in 8-inch layer-cake pan. Add mixture. Bake in moderate oven (375°F.) until top is golden brown, 30 to 40 minutes. Serve warm. Cut in wedges or squares.

To reheat, sprinkle with 2 tablespoons water and place in preheated 350°F. oven, letting it warm *slowly* but thoroughly. SERVES 8.

Spinach Pie [*Fritada de Espinaca*]

1 pound spinach
2 eggs
4 tablespoons cottage cheese
2 tablespoons grated Romano cheese
1 medium-sized boiled potato, mashed
  Salt to taste
4 tablespoons olive oil

Wash spinach, drain thoroughly, and cut into small

pieces. Add the eggs, cottage cheese, Romano cheese, potato, and salt. Mix well and place in oiled cake pan as in
Leek Pie, above.

Bake 10 minutes in moderate oven (350°F.).
SERVES 6.

Lentils

Lentils prepared this way are served with white rice
(Pilaf, page 104), each person at the table taking the
proportion of pilaf with lentils he desires. A small piece
of boiled or potted beef completes the entree.

½ onion, diced
2 tablespoons olive oil
2 cups beef stock
½ cup tomato sauce
1 cup lentils
1 teaspoon salt

In a small skillet sauté the onion till pale gold. Cool. In
a saucepan bring stock and tomato sauce to a boil. Add
onion, with olive oil in which it was sautéed. Add the
lentils and salt. Cover, and cook over low heat till the
lentils are tender and the stock absorbed, about 1 hour. If
stock is absorbed before the lentils are done, add more
stock or water. Serve hot. SERVES 4.

Okra à la Smyrna [*Bamies*]

GREECE

Young, small okra (1½ to 2 inches long) should be used
for this recipe.

      1 pound okra
 1½ cups stock or water
      2 tablespoons olive oil
      2 tablespoons tomato sauce
 1½ teaspoons salt
      1 tablespoon lemon juice

Wash okra, cut off stem ends, and place in hot water for
2 minutes. Drain.

Put stock or water, olive oil, and tomato sauce in a
shallow pan and bring to a boil; then add okra and salt
and finally the lemon juice. Cook until tender. Brown
lightly under broiler before serving. SERVES 6.

When sun-ripened tomatoes are available, add 2
medium-sized tomatoes cut in eighths to the okra while
cooking.

Onions and Chick Peas
[*Cebollas con Garbanzos*]

SPAIN

      1 pound small white onions, uniform size
      1 cup stock or water
      2 tablespoons tomato sauce
      2 tablespoons olive oil
          Salt and pepper
      1 tablespoon lemon juice
      2 ounces or 2 chunks leftover beef (optional)
      ½ cup canned or parboiled chick peas

Peel and wash onions. Plunge into boiling water for 5
minutes. Drain. Combine and cook stock or water, to-

mato sauce, olive oil, salt and pepper. When blended, add the onions and lemon juice. Cook 20 minutes or until tender.

When halfway finished, stir in the chick peas, which have been drained. Complete cooking on low heat. Serve hot. SERVES 6.

Peas and Pods [*Ervias con Vainas*]

SPAIN

2 pounds green peas in pods
1 cup chicken broth or water
2 tablespoons olive oil
½ teaspoon salt

Shell peas, setting aside about 1 dozen young green pods for use with vegetable. Carefully peel off skin from inner side of pod and discard, leaving the succulent outer portion. Break into ¾-inch pieces and add to peas.

Bring broth and olive oil to a boil in a saucepan. Add peas and prepared pods.

Cook briskly. When tender, add salt and serve. SERVES 6.

NOTE: If peas are a bit old, add a carrot or a pinch of sugar. The pods add a unique flavor to the peas.

Green Peppers [*Peperoni Verdi*]

ITALY

1 pound green peppers
4 tablespoons olive oil

Remove seeds and cut peppers in ¾-inch wide strips. In hot olive oil ¼ inch deep, sauté peppers until tender. Drain on brown paper and serve hot. SERVES 6.

Potatoes à la Smyrna

This is a change from the usual methods of preparing potatoes which will add interest to a routine meal.

> 1 pound potatoes
> 2 tablespoons olive oil
> 1 teaspoon salt
> 2 tablespoons tomato sauce

Peel or scrape, wash, and quarter potatoes; drain. In a small skillet, brown potatoes lightly in hot olive oil. Then add salt to 3 cups water and tomato sauce, which have been brought to a boil. Add the olive oil and the browned potatoes. Cook briskly. When finished, most of the liquid should be absorbed and a light gravy formed. Serve hot. SERVES 4.

Potatoes with Onions à la Smyrna

> 1 pound (3 medium-sized) potatoes
> ⅓ cup olive oil
> 1 large onion, thinly sliced
>   Salt and pepper
> 1 tablespoon minced Italian parsley

Wash potatoes well and cook in jackets in salted water till tender. Meanwhile heat olive oil in skillet. Add onion and sauté till limp but not brown. Peel potatoes and cut into ½-inch slices. Stir into the onion without mashing. Season and sprinkle with minced parsley. SERVES 4.

Potato Balls [Buñuelos]

Generally used for breakfast or lunch—served with honey, maple or sugar syrup.

        2 potatoes, cooked and mashed
        ½ cup grated Romano cheese or Parmesan
        ⅓ cup cracker meal
        2 eggs
           Salt to taste

Beat eggs well, add the rest of the ingredients. Stir thoroughly till batter is smooth. Drop batter quickly from a large serving spoon (equivalent of 2 tablespoons) into deep boiling olive oil, until all batter is used up. Reduce heat. When brown, remove and drain. (The olive oil can be strained and used again.) Serve warm with sugar syrup. SERVES 4.

SUGAR SYRUP

        ½ cup sugar
        1 cup water
        2 teaspoons lemon juice

Bring all ingredients to a boil, simmer for 15 minutes or until right consistency. May be used plain or with cinnamon to taste.

Boiled Spinach or Escarole

Twist off roots or coarse stems of vegetable. Place in water, then lift out leaves, allowing grit to settle. After 3 or 4 washings, drain off excess water in colander.

Cover bottom of pan with about 4 tablespoons of water, heat, add spinach, and let cook 4 to 8 minutes. (Escarole requires more time and consequently more liquid.) When tender, add salt.

Serve cool with olive oil and lemon juice.

Spinach in Broth [*Spinaci in Brodo*]

ITALY

1 pound spinach
1½ cups chicken broth
Salt to taste

Prepare spinach as in first paragraph of previous recipe. Bring broth to a boil; add spinach. Cook until tender, 4 to 8 minutes. SERVES 6.

Spinach with Rice and Cheese, Greek Style [*Spanokorizo*]

1 pound spinach
2 tablespoons olive oil
¾ cup uncooked rice or 2 cups cooked rice
¼ tablespoon Kash Kaval cheese, sliced

Wash spinach as in Boiled Spinach or Escarole (page 95). Drain. Then cook with ⅓ cup water and the olive oil.

Cook uncooked rice in a small saucepan with ¾ cup water.

When the rice is done but not mushy, stir it into the spinach and the liquid in which the spinach has cooked. Then add cheese and simmer for 10 minutes. Serve with yoghurt. SERVES 6.

This is a good dish to serve for lunch.

Spinach with Beans
[*Habas con Espinaca*]

SPAIN

This dish, combined with rice, is an agreeable substitute for the stereotyped meal and a favorite among Eastern Mediterranean people. It is most welcome on a cold day.

    ¾ cup dried cannellini beans (marrow beans)
    1 pound spinach, washed
    1 large marrow bone or ¼ pound parboiled or
          leftover beef
    6 tablespoons olive oil
    1 teaspoon salt
    2 cups stock or water

Cover beans with water and soak overnight, or keep in tepid water for about 6 hours.

Pick over beans. Cook vigorously, starting with cold water, for about an hour. Place one-half the spinach in saucepan or shallow casserole, then a layer of half the

beans, with the marrow bone or beef. Repeat layers, using the rest of the spinach and beans. Add olive oil and
2 cups water. Cook for 15 minutes. When the beans are
tender, add salt. Avoid overcooking to prevent beans
from falling apart. Serve hot in soup dishes. SERVES 6.

Grilled Tomatoes

    6 firm medium-sized tomatoes
    ½ teaspoon salt
    ¼ teaspoon pepper
    ¼ teaspoon oregano
    ¼ teaspoon minced garlic (optional)
    1 tablespoon olive oil
    1 tablespoon grated bread or cracker meal

Wash tomatoes and cut in half crosswise. Place in shallow
casserole, cut side up. Blend seasonings with olive oil and
pour over the tomatoes. Place in oven preheated to
350°F. Bake for 15 to 20 minutes. Sprinkle bread crumbs
over top and brown lightly under the broiler. Serve hot.
SERVES 6.

Tomato Pie [*Fritada de Tomate*]

    1½ pounds tomatoes
     2 slices of stale white bread
    ¾ cup coarsely chopped parsley
     3 eggs, beaten
       Salt and pepper to taste
     1 cup grated Romano cheese
    ¼ cup olive oil

Cut tomatoes in small chunks. Press juice out through a colander. Soak the bread in the juice.

In a bowl mix all the ingredients except the olive oil and reserving ¼ cup cheese.

Heat the olive oil slightly in a nine-inch cake pan. Rotate so that the sides are oiled. Pour the mixture into the pan. Sprinkle top with the remaining cheese.

Bake in oven preheated to 400°F. for ½ hour. Reduce heat to 300°F., bake an additional 30 to 40 minutes until brown. Serve warm. SERVES 6.

Zucchini

Young zucchini (¾ to 1 inch in diameter) is best for the following recipes. When squash is older (1½ to 2 inches in diameter) it is better to use them for stuffing or for the Zucchini Pudding, p. 100.

Boiled Zucchini

(But not insipid)

    1 pound small, firm zucchini
1½ tablespoons olive oil
    1 clove garlic
       Salt
    1 tablespoon lemon juice
       Pepper

Wash the zucchini; scrape the skin off and cut zucchini into 2-inch strips.

Bring ¾ cup water, olive oil, and garlic to a boil, add salt and zucchini. Cook briskly 3 to 6 minutes, till tender but not mushy. Remove garlic. Add lemon juice and pepper to taste. Serve cool. SERVES 6.

Zucchini Provençal

Follow directions for Boiled Zucchini, above, substituting 2 tablespoons tomato sauce for the lemon juice. Serve hot. SERVES 6.

Variation: When zucchini is tender, transfer to a shallow casserole, sprinkle with 2 tablespoons grated Parmesan cheese, and brown lightly under broiler. Serve hot.

Fried Zucchini

Be sure zucchini is young to obtain best results. Wash the zucchini; scrape off the skin and cut the vegetable into thin discs or 2-inch strips. Sprinkle with flour and fry in hot (not smoking) olive oil until golden brown. Sprinkle with salt and serve.

For variety dip in flour and beaten egg, and fry in deep hot olive oil.

Zucchini Pudding
[*Fritada de Calabasa*]

        2 pounds zucchini or yellow squash (1½
               inches in diameter)
        3 tablespoons bread crumbs
     1½ teaspoons salt
        ¼ teaspoon pepper
        4 eggs
        ½ cup grated Parmesan cheese

Wash, scrape, and grate the zucchini. In a colander or
coarse strainer squeeze out excess water.

In a bowl mix the zucchini thoroughly with the rest
of the ingredients, reserving 3 tablespoons of the cheese.
Transfer to well-oiled 9-inch casserole. Sprinkle top with
remaining cheese. Bake in hot oven, preheated to 450°F.,
reducing heat to 350°F. after 15 minutes. Let it bake for
15 to 20 minutes longer till it is brown. Serve hot. To
reheat, sprinkle with a very little water (1 tablespoon)
and warm in moderate oven, preheated to 325°F.
SERVES 6.

Zucchini or Yellow Squash
Casserole

        1 pound zucchini or yellow squash
        2 tablespoons olive oil
        1 teaspoon salt

Pepper to taste
Grated Parmesan cheese
Sliced Fontina cheese

Scrape and wash zucchini and cut into ¼-inch slices. Arrange in 3 to 4 layers in a casserole previously greased with olive oil. Sprinkle each layer with salt, pepper, and grated cheese.

Bake for 25 minutes in oven preheated to 350°F. Add sliced Fontina cheese and bake for additional 5 to 8 minutes until cheese melts. Serve immediately. SERVES 4.

Squash and Eggplant

1 ¾-pound eggplant
1 ¾-pound squash
1 medium onion, chopped
  Salt and pepper to taste
¼ cup tomato sauce
3 tablespoons olive oil
¼ teaspoon sugar

Peel, wash, and cut the eggplant and squash into 2-inch pieces. Add the other ingredients and cook together in a saucepan on low heat until well blended and the texture of marmalade. Serve hot. SERVES 6.

Casserole of Vegetables [Yuvetch]

This is a popular Turkish one-dish meal. White rice is the traditional accompaniment to this in Turkey. In

Latin American countries, 1½ cups of diced potatoes are added to the casserole instead of serving with rice.

    1 small eggplant
    ½ pound young squash, green or yellow
    1 green pepper, seeded
    1 large onion
    ¼ cup tomato sauce
    4 tablespoons olive oil
    1½ to 2 pounds chuck steak
    1½ cups canned tomatoes, drained and chopped
    ¼ cup coarsely cut parsley
       Salt and pepper to taste
    1 4-ounce can peas, drained

Cut meat into 3 or 4 strips, sauté in hot olive oil, add 1 cup of water, simmer for ½ hour. Cut eggplant, squash and pepper into 1-inch squares and onion into thin slivers. Place in top-of-stove casserole with tomato sauce and 1 cup of liquid from the drained tomatoes. Cook briskly for 15 minutes. Place the strips of meat over the vegetables and add the sauce. Then add the chopped to-matoes, parsley, salt and pepper. Reduce heat. Let sim-mer slowly an additional 20 minutes. Do not stir; test for doneness with fork. When almost ready cover with peas. Cook additional 5 minutes. Serve immediately. SERVES 8.

> *Mrs. M. Amateau, Island of Rhodes*
> *and Constantinople*

Grains and Pasta

Bulgur

Bulgur (cracked wheat), like *arroz* (long-grained rice) or *fideos* (vermicelli), adds such an unusual note to a routine menu that our guests invariably are as stimulated and pleased as if they had accompanied us on a sea trip to an exotic destination. And actually they have, for these dishes do come from remote and curious places!

        1 medium onion, diced
        3 tablespoons olive oil
    2½ cups beef or chicken broth
        1 teaspoon salt
        1 cup bulgur

Sauté onion in hot olive oil in a saucepan till light brown. Cool and add broth. Bring to a boil. Add salt and bulgur. When the combined contents come to a boil, cover, reduce heat, and let cook for 30 minutes. (A fine-grain bulgur requires less time.) Remove lid to allow escape of steam. Serve hot. SERVES 6.

Rice Pilaf, Greek Style

Rice, correctly prepared, with the kernels separate, adds a delightful fillip to a meal.

    5 tablespoons olive oil
    1 cup chicken or beef broth, or water
    1 teaspoon salt
    1 cup white rice

NOTE: It is important to use a shallow 8-inch saucepan no deeper than 3 to 4 inches.

Heat olive oil in saucepan on medium heat until it browns a small piece of bread. Cool and then add the broth or water. (If you use water, brown a clove of garlic in the olive oil and discard garlic.) Bring to a boil; add salt and then the rice, which has been washed carefully. When this mixture has boiled briskly for 2 to 3 minutes, cover, reduce heat, and cook for 15 minutes. By this time the rice should be tender but firm. Uncover and allow steam to escape. The tradition is to serve the rice piping hot on a platter, thus displaying the separate grains.

In order to regulate the cooking heat it may be necessary to use an asbestos pad under the saucepan.

Serve rice plain, with grated cheese, or with pine nuts browned in olive oil. SERVES 6.

Rice with Chick Peas [*Ceci con Riso*]

    ½ cup canned or parboiled chick peas
    1 tablespoon olive oil

½ teaspoon salt
¼ teaspoon pepper
1 cup white or red rice

Drain liquid from chick peas. Add olive oil, salt, and pepper. Prepare rice as for Rice Pilaf, above, but when the rice is parboiled stir in the peas. Continue cooking as for Rice Pilaf. Serve hot. SERVES 6.

Red Rice [*Arroz Rojo*]

Although it is called red rice, the rice is really a delicate salmon color.

5 tablespoons olive oil
1 cup chicken or beef broth or water
2 tablespoons tomato sauce or 2 teaspoons
    tomato paste
1 teaspoon salt
1 cup long-grained rice

NOTE: It is important to use shallow saucepan or casserole about four inches deep.

Heat olive oil on medium heat until it browns a small piece of bread. Discard bread. When the olive oil has cooled, add the broth and tomato sauce or paste. Bring to a boil and add the salt and then the rice. When the mixture has boiled briskly for 2 to 3 minutes, cover, reduce heat, and cook for 15 minutes. By this time the rice should be tender but firm. Uncover, and allow steam to escape.

When cooking twice the quantity, leave uncovered for 5 minutes, when the rice starts to boil, before covering and reducing the heat. SERVES 6.

White Rice with Turkish Dressing

    1 small onion, sliced
    ½ green pepper, seeded and sliced in semicircles
    3 tablespoons olive oil
    2 pimientos, shredded
    1 cup stock or water
    1 teaspoon salt
    1 cup white rice
    1 8-ounce can of small peas

Sauté onion and green pepper in olive oil in a saucepan till limp. Add pimientos and stock or water. Simmer till blended, 5 to 10 minutes. Bring to a boil and proceed as for Rice Pilaf, page 104. When the rice is done, add the peas, drained, and serve hot. SERVES 6.

Persian Garnish for White Rice

    2 tablespoons olive oil
    1 medium onion, sliced
    1 tablespoon blanched almonds, split
        lengthwise
    2 tablespoons pine nuts

Heat olive oil in a 6-inch skillet. Add the onion. When limp, add the almonds and finally the pine nuts. Fry all till golden brown. Serve hot on white rice. SERVES 6.

Spaghetti

Spaghetti tastes best to the connoisseur when cooked *al dente*—firm to the teeth. The time of cooking varies according to the type of grain from which the spaghetti is made, as well as the thickness of the pasta.

Cook vigorously in a generous amount of boiling salted water. Test after 5 minutes between thumb and forefinger. Boil till tender but still firm.

Spaghetti with Butter
[*Spaghetti al Burro*]

This is the simplest and quickest form of spaghetti. Have soup plates ready with 1 tablespoon butter in each. As soon as the spaghetti, which has been boiled in salted water, is ready, lift with a fork from the pot into the individual soup plates. In this way whatever water clings to the spaghetti combines with the melting butter to form a palatable sauce. Serve immediately. Add grated cheese at table.

Spaghetti with Garlic
[*Spaghetti con Aglio*]

¾ pound spaghetti
1 clove garlic
3 tablespoons olive oil

Boil spaghetti as directed on page 107. Cut clove of garlic into 4 parts. Brown in olive oil, being sure not to burn the oil. Discard garlic. Pour olive oil into a large heated bowl. When the spaghetti is ready (*al dente*), drain in colander and turn it into the heated bowl, tossing it well to distribute the flavored olive oil. Serve hot immediately and add grated cheese at table as desired.

The flavor may be varied by adding 1 tablespoon unheated olive oil to mixture.

Leftover spaghetti may be used a day or two later in one of the casserole recipes.

Spaghetti in Casserole, Meatless

    ¾ cup sliced onion
    3 tablespoons olive oil
    4 eggs
    4 tablespoons grated Parmesan cheese
    ¾ pound spaghetti
    2 teaspoons butter

Sauté onion in olive oil until limp. Drain, using surplus olive oil to grease baking pan. In a bowl, mix sautéed onion, beaten eggs, and 3 tablespoons grated cheese. Add spaghetti, which has been boiled and drained, to egg mixture.

Stir thoroughly, pour into greased 9-inch baking pan, and bake in moderate oven till egg is firm. Dot with butter and sprinkle with remaining cheese, or brush with beaten egg. Brown under broiler. Serve hot. SERVES 6.

This mixture may also be cooked in a saucepan on top of the stove. Then it is necessary to stir frequently to prevent sticking. It will have a loose, tossed texture.

Spaghetti in Casserole, with Meat

Follow directions in the preceding recipe, adding ¼ pound chopped meat to the eggs. Add sautéed onion to the mixture and add cheese if desired. Proceed as above.

Spaghettini alla Marinara

    2 large onions, cut in slices and quartered
    ½ cup olive oil
    1 clove garlic
    3 cups strained Italian plum tomatoes, or
           1½ cups tomato sauce and 1 cup water
    ⅓ cup chopped parsley
    ¼ teaspoon dried mushroom
    1 teaspoon salt
    ½ teaspoon freshly ground pepper
    1 pound spaghettini

Sauté onions in olive oil till light brown. Add garlic, minced, or cut in half to be discarded when brown. Cool, add tomatoes or tomato sauce and water. Bring to a boil. Add meat if desired. Simmer for 20 minutes. Add parsley, dried mushroom broken up, salt, and freshly ground pepper. Let mixture simmer for an additional 10 minutes. If tomatoes are very watery, cook until sauce has desired consistency. Serve with freshly prepared spaghettini. A fresh ripe tomato cut into small pieces may be added to the sauce while simmering. SERVES 6.

Aunt Rose's Spaghettini and Meat Casserole

    ¾ pound spaghettini
    3 eggs
    ½ pound chopped beef
       Salt and pepper
    ¼ cup olive oil
    2 scant tablespoons cracker crumbs or grated
          cheese (optional)

Boil spaghettini in salted water and drain in colander, reserving 3 tablespoons water. Mix in a bowl with 2 eggs. Mix together the meat, 1 egg, seasoning, and water from spaghettini.

Heat olive oil gently in a 10-inch pan or shallow casserole. Place layer of spaghettini mixture, then a layer of meat mixture. Repeat. Sprinkle top with cracker crumbs or cheese if desired. Bake in oven preheated to 350°F. for 35 minutes. Serve piping hot. SERVES 6.

Toasted Fettuccine in Tomato Sauce [*Fila*]

½ pound fettuccine (1 ¼ inch wide)
¼ cup olive oil
4 tablespoons tomato sauce
3 cups stock or water
1 teaspoon salt

Preheat oven to 375°F. Place fettuccine in oven on a cooky sheet till lightly browned. Heat olive oil till it will brown a crumb of bread. Discard bread. Cool olive oil and add tomato sauce, stock or water, and salt. Bring to a boil and add the fettuccine. Cover and cook briskly 8 to 10 minutes, until the liquid is absorbed and pasta is tender but not mushy. Remove lid to permit escape of steam. Stir with fork before serving. SERVES 4.

Fideos (vermicelli) may also be prepared in this manner.

Fettuccine and Peas

1 pound fettuccine
1 tablespoon butter
1 pound fresh peas, cooked in salted water,
      or 1 8-ounce can peas
3 tablespoons grated Parmesan cheese

Boil fettuccine as you do spaghetti, page 107, being sure

to cook *al dente*. Add the butter to the hot drained fettuccine, allowing it to melt, forming a sauce. Add the
peas. Serve hot. Sprinkle with cheese at the table. SERVES
6.

Vermicelli [*Fideos*]

Vermicelli, or *fideos*, as prepared in the following recipe,
is a unique dish which we have encountered in only one
area of the Mediterranean—among the Sephardic Jews
of Smyrna. Nevertheless, it is one of the most *well-liked*
dishes we have served, and never fails to evoke most enthusiastic comment. It seems to add excitement to the
most unpretentious menu.

   ½ cup olive oil
   8 ounces vermicelli
1½ cups stock or water
   2 tablespoons tomato sauce
   1 teaspoon salt

Heat olive oil in small skillet until a crumb of bread
can be lightly browned. Then take the vermicelli and
brown very lightly, 3 or 4 "twists" at a time. As soon
as they are a light brown, remove. Repeat until all vermicelli twists are brown. Bring stock or water, sauce, and
2 tablespoons of the remaining olive oil to a boil in a shallow saucepan or casserole (about 4 inches deep). Add salt
and the browned twists of vermicelli. Cover and cook
for 8 to 10 minutes till tender but not mushy. Stir once
with a fork without breaking the strands. When vermicelli is done, remove lid to permit escape of steam. Serve
hot. SERVES 4 TO 6.

Tagliatelli with Green Sauce
[*Pesto Genovese*]

2 cups fresh basil leaves (free of stems)
1 clove garlic
1 tablespoon butter
3 tablespoons olive oil
20 pine nuts (2 ounces)
⅔ cup grated Parmesan cheese and ⅓ cup
    grated Sardo cheese or 1 cup grated
    Parmesan cheese
1 tablespoon milk
1 pound tagliatelli

Whirl first five ingredients in blender. Add Parmesan and Sardo cheese and milk and whirl again. Sauce should be the consistency of purée. If necessary, add a tablespoon of the water in which the tagliatelli is cooked.

Cook tagliatelli as you do spaghetti, page 107. Pour sauce over hot, freshly cooked tagliatelli. SERVES 4.

Desserts

Apple Pie

Of course, this is strictly an American-English dessert.
The Mediterranean touch is supplied when the crust is
prepared with olive oil. And what enthusiasm this
arouses! Confirmed dessert dodgers have eaten our pies
with delight.

          2 cups sifted flour
             Salt
       ¾ cup olive oil
          2 pounds apples, about 6 apples
          2 teaspoons cinnamon
       ½ cup sugar

Put the sifted flour in a bowl, add salt, and with a fork
stir in the olive oil and ¼ cup cold water, adding half
at a time. Stir lightly. Divide in half and roll lightly
between palms. Refrigerate while preparing the apples.

Peel, core, and cut apples into wedges ⅜ inch thick.
Take one ball of dough and roll from center out on board
(between sheets of wax paper, if you like). Sprinkle
lightly with flour. Place in pie pan, fitting it around.
Arrange slices of apples all around crust, heaping higher

in center. Roll out the second ball of dough until large enough to place over the apples.

Blend remaining flour, about a heaping tablespoon, with cinnamon, ½ cup sugar, and ½ teaspoon salt. Stir well. The mixture should be sweet, but not too sweet. Sprinkle in among wedges of apple and over them. Pick up dough from board and lay it over the heaped wedges. Seal around the edge and scallop the edge of the dough with your fingers, or flute with a fork.

To glaze crust (optional), apply white of egg with brush or three fingers.

Place in oven preheated to 350°F. In 25 minutes increase to 400°F. for 15 to 20 minutes. SERVES 6 TO 8.

Apricot Meringue [*Kavisi*]

(Simplified)

         2 cups pitted fresh apricots
         1 tablespoon lemon juice
      1½ cups sugar
         1 cup ground almonds
        ½ cup pine nuts, mashed or pounded
         3 to 4 tablespoons sweet sherry
         3 egg whites
        ¾ teaspoon cream of tartar
         6 tablespoons sugar

Put the pitted apricots and lemon juice in a saucepan and cook on low heat until much of the liquid is extracted from the fruit. Stir in 1 cup of the sugar until dissolved. Cook for 30 minutes over low heat, stirring frequently. Then put aside to cool.

Mix ½ cup each of the ground almonds, sugar, and

mashed or pounded pine nuts with just enough sherry to make a soft paste. Fill the apricots with this mixture. Arrange in a greased glass baking dish and sprinkle the rest of the ground almonds over them.

Beat the egg whites with 6 tablespoons of sugar and the cream of tartar until they are stiff. Spread over the apricots and almond paste. Bake meringue in a preheated slow oven (300°F.) until it is firm and lightly browned. Serve warm. SERVES 6 TO 8.

If canned apricots are used instead of fresh ones, no sugar or cooking is required.

Apricot Whip

½ pound dried apricots
⅓ cup sugar
½ teaspoon lemon juice
4 egg whites

Wash fruit and cook in just enough water to soften. Rub through a coarse strainer. Add sugar and cook 5 minutes or until the mixture has the consistency of marmalade; to this add the lemon juice. Fold this mixture into the stiffly beaten whites of eggs. Heap lightly in a greased pan or casserole, 3 to 4 inches deep, and bake 30 to 40 minutes in a slow oven, 275°F. Serve cool with cream. SERVES 6.

Date Whip

Follow recipe for Apricot Whip, substituting dried pitted dates for the apricots, eliminating the sugar, and using 1 teaspoon lemon juice. SERVES 6.

Prune Whip

Follow recipe for Apricot Whip, substituting dried prunes for the apricots. If sour prunes (Oregon prunes) are used, eliminate lemon juice. SERVES 6.

Banana Flambé [*Plátanos Flambeados*]

      6 bananas
      6 tablespoons butter or olive oil
      6 tablespoons granulated sugar
    1½ teaspoons cinnamon or grated lemon rind
    12 tablespoons (6 ounces) Crème de Cacao or
            a cordial
    12 tablespoons Cognac

Peel the bananas and cut in half lengthwise. If small leave whole. Melt the butter in a frying pan. In it sautée the bananas till a golden brown. In the same pan or in a chafing dish, cover the banana with the sugar blended with cinnamon or lemon rind, and Crème de Cacao. At the table pour the Cognac over the banana and light it. When the flame subsides, serve. SERVES 6.

Compote, Athenian Style

To a mixture of stewed or canned pears, apples, plums, and prunes, add shredded, Preserved Orange Peel (see below)—about four strands per individual portion. This not only transforms a bland dish into a piquant dessert, but also provides the additional vitamin value found in the rind.

PRESERVED ORANGE PEEL

Peel of 1 navel orange removed in 3 or 4
sections
½ cup sugar

Wash peels and shred with sharp knife into ⅛-inch strips. Place peels in saucepan, cover with cold water, bring to a boil, and drain. Repeat five times. Heat the sugar with ¼ cup hot water. When dissolved, add the drained orange peel, letting it cook slowly until the syrup is almost entirely evaporated. Put in covered, scalded jar till ready for use.

If the strips are cut thicker, ¼ inch, they may be rolled in granulated sugar and served as candy.

Blackberry Sponge

1 tablespoon unflavored gelatin
1 cup hot blackberry juice
2 tablespoons lemon juice
¾ cup brown sugar
2 egg whites
¼ cup fresh blackberries
1 cup whipped cream

Sprinkle gelatin on ¼ cup cold water to soften. Stir in the blackberry juice, lemon juice, and sugar. Cool, stirring occasionally. When partly set, beat with a rotary beater till frothy. Beat the egg whites till they are stiff. Fold in, then beat entire mixture until it is stiff.

Heap into sherbet glasses. Chill for a few hours. Serve with fresh blackberries and whipped cream. SERVES 6.

Stewed Peaches

Select firm fruit. Wash and immerse in boiling water for 3 to 5 minutes. Remove skin, and cover peaches with the water used for scalding. Add 1 teaspoon sugar for each peach and cook 15 to 25 minutes or until tender. Serve cool.

One ¼-inch strip of lemon rind cooked with peaches varies the flavor agreeably.

Stewed Pears

6 Anjou or large brown pears
3 tablespoons sugar or honey
1 lemon

Wash and peel pears, leaving stem but scooping out the dark part of the blossom end. Cover with water and cook till tender but still firm. Use only enough sugar to sweeten the liquid. When almost finished, add 2 to 3 wedges of lemon. Serve cold.

Pears, Roman Style

Prepare fruit as for Stewed Pears, above. When fruit is parboiled arrange in a shallow casserole and cover each pear with a mixture of equal parts of honey, the liquid in which the fruit was cooked, and a sweet or medium-dry wine. Place casserole in oven preheated to 400°F. and allow to glaze for 10 to 15 minutes. Baste from time to time. Serve cold.

The flavor of the fruit is enhanced if some of the peel, thoroughly washed, is cooked with the pears.

Pomegranate

One of the happiest recollections of my childhood in England was the celebration of the harvest season with pomegranates shipped from the Mediterranean countries. Transplanted to America, we continued the custom even though pomegranates were quite hard to come by.

Years later, when I accompanied my husband on business trips to Spain, our hosts and friends observed my delight at the sight of the pomegranate tree and its beautiful fruit. Since then they never miss the opportunity of serving my favorite dessert. There, the custom is to remove the gemlike seeds from the peel and heap the sparkling fruit in a crystal bowl. The Andalusian pomegranate literally melts in your mouth! They say you have to put on a raincoat when you peel the fruit, but it is well worth the effort!

To a child—well or ill—the pomegranate represents adventure and a wonderful reward.

Quince [*Membrillo*]

Quince has a unique and subtle flavor. It is very popular in Mediterranean and South American countries and it deserves a wider use in our country. It is served as a stewed fruit or as jam.

Stewed Quince

1 pound quince
   Sugar
   Juice of 1 lemon
1 plum (optional)

Wash and peel fruit and cut in eighths or one-inch cubes. Cover with water and cook until tender, adding water if necessary. When almost tender, add sugar to taste. Let cook till water partially evaporates, leaving a syrupy sauce. Add lemon juice and serve cool. A small blue plum cut up and added while mixture is cooking gives an even richer color. SERVES 6.

Quince Preserves

Choose ripe quince, wash, and immerse in boiling water. Bring to a boil in the water once; peel, remove the core, and put fruit through a coarse strainer. Place in a kettle with an equal weight of sugar and juice of 1 lemon. Cook till the preserves are the texture of marmalade, about 15 to 20 minutes; stir constantly, being sure to stir the contents from the bottom of the pot. When thoroughly cooked, pour into a large bowl or mold or into individual molds. Serve cold.

A second method: To 2¼ cups of sugar add 2 cups of water. Boil until mixture has dissolved and is syrupy. Then add it to the strained quince. No further cooking is needed.

Rhubarb

Rhubarb prepared with root of ginger or wedges of the small Seville-type orange has a mellow and unusual flavor.

Wash rhubarb and cut off leaves and stem ends. Peel unless tender. Cut into 1-inch pieces. Add ⅓ as much sugar, just enough water to keep from burning, root of ginger cut into 1-inch pieces or 2 wedges of orange to 1 pound of rhubarb. Cook till tender. A heatproof glass or enamel saucepan is suggested.

Strawberries

In southern European countries the small wild strawberries are served with orange juice as dessert. We can serve our small berries in the same manner.

Custard with Caramel Sauce [*Flan*]

    2 eggs
       Pinch of salt
    2 tablespoons sugar
    ½ teaspoon vanilla or lemon extract
    1 pint hot milk

Beat eggs slightly; add salt, sugar, and flavoring, stirring until dissolved. Pour milk gradually into eggs and stir. Pour Caramel Sauce (see below) into custard cups or mold. Then add custard. Place cups in a pan of hot water, put pan in a moderate oven (325°F.), and bake 30 to 45 minutes. Test with a knife. If the knife comes out clean, the custard is done. Serve cold. SERVES 4.

CARAMEL SAUCE

In a small pan, put 3 tablespoons sugar. Place over low heat, adding about 6 drops of lemon juice, and stir with a wooden spoon until it becomes dark brown and a foam forms at the top.

Rice Pudding [*Sootlatch*]

TURKEY

Rice pudding, decorated with cinnamon, may be served cool as a dessert or breakfast dish.

    ½ cup short-grained rice
    ¼ teaspoon salt
    1 quart milk
    1 tablespoon sugar
       Cinnamon

Place rice in 1½ cups cold water with salt, bring to a boil, then simmer till soft. Add milk and sugar and cook slowly until the mixture is thick and creamy, stirring every 10 to 15 minutes. Pour into dessert dishes. When cool, sprinkle cinnamon on top. Chill and serve cold. SERVES 6.

Yoghurt

1 quart milk
4 to 6 teaspoons previously made yoghurt to
      be used as culture

Heat milk to 110°F. or slightly warmer than the inside
of wrist. (Greek housewives test with the second joint
of the little finger.) Pour into a bowl and add the previously made yoghurt.

Or blend in a cup the yoghurt culture with an equal
amount of the tepid milk and then stir into the bowl.

Set in warm place away from drafts, or set in a pan
of hot water in the oven, for 10 hours or overnight.
When the yoghurt is the proper consistency, cover with
cheesecloth and drain off whey. Add fruit flavoring, if
desired. Refrigerate. SERVES 6.

Cookies, Confections, and Holiday Treats

Almond Brittle

SMYRNA

2 cups almonds
2 cups granulated sugar
1 tablespoon lemon juice

Place almonds in boiling water. After 2 minutes drain, remove skins, cut in half lengthwise, and roast in oven preheated to 350°F. till dry and crisp.

Heat the sugar in a small skillet till it melts, add the almonds, stirring continuously until the mixture is heated through. Stir in the lemon juice.

Grease a glass or heatproof dish with butter or olive oil. Spread the candy mixture. Then cut it into 2-inch squares.

Amelia Azecri, Smyrna

Candied Grapefruit Rind
[*Kitra Glykisma Zacharomeno*]

GREECE

Just as tea is offered to the guest in an English house-hold, so is Dulce de Portugal or de Pomelo offered as soon as a visitor crosses the threshold of a Greek or Turkish home. This is immediately followed with aromatic Turkish coffee served with a beautiful foam atop each dainty cup. Then relaxed conversation and a state of euphoria prevail!

    2 grapefruit with fleshy rind
    2¾ cups sugar
    2 tablespoons lemon juice

Peel grapefruit, cutting the rind into 1-inch pieces. Soak in cold water for two hours. Bring 3 cups water and sugar to a boil and cook briskly for 10 minutes. Drain and squeeze the grapefruit peel dry. Add to syrup. Pour lemon juice over mixture. Continue cooking for about ½ hour until the juice is syrupy. Serve cool. MAKES 20 PIECES.

Stuffed Figs

    1 pound Smyrna or California figs
    ½ pound walnuts
    1 pound almonds

Roast nuts, as on page 4. Stuff the figs with shelled walnuts or almonds, or a combination of both.

Turkish Coffee Cake [*Rosca*]

> 1 package dry yeast
> 3 cups flour
> 3 tablespoons sugar
> ½ teaspoon cinnamon
> 2 eggs
> 1 tablespoon olive oil
> ½ cup sesame seeds

Dissolve yeast in 1 cup warm water. In a mixing bowl put flour, sugar, cinnamon, one egg, and olive oil. Stir well. Knead the dough, gradually adding the dissolved yeast. Continue kneading till the dough is smooth and shiny.

Divide dough into four equal parts. Roll each part into a strip about 8 to 10 inches long and form each into a ring. Cover with a tea towel and blanket and set aside in a warm place for an hour in order to rise. Before baking, brush with beaten egg and sprinkle on the sesame seeds. Bake in oven preheated to 375°F. for about 25 minutes, or until golden brown. SERVES 8 TO 12.

Almond Bread

> 3 eggs
> ⅔ cup sugar
>   Juice and grated rind of 1 medium-sized lemon
> ¾ teaspoon vanilla or grated vanilla bean
> 3 cups flour
> 3 teaspoons baking powder
>   Scant ½ cup olive oil
> ½ cup blanched almonds

Beat eggs well; add sugar and beat together. Add lemon juice and grated rind, vanilla, and 1 cup of flour which has been sifted with the baking powder. Add the almonds, cut in half lengthwise. Add the olive oil and the rest of the flour. Knead into 2 long loaves about 2 inches wide. Place on oiled and floured pan. Bake loaves in a slow oven (325°F.) for 20 to 30 minutes. Remove the loaves from the pan and, while they are still warm, cut them into ½-inch slices. Lay the slices out on pans and place in oven at 250°F. to be lightly browned. When cool, store in cooky jars.

Sesame Seed Cookies [*Reshikahs*]

(Aunt Victoria's method)

    4 eggs
    ¼ teaspoon cinnamon or 1 teaspoon vanilla
    4 cups flour plus enough to facilitate rolling
         the dough
    2 teaspoons baking powder
    ½ cup olive oil
    ¾ cup sugar
    2 tablespoons milk
    ½ cup sesame seeds

Beat eggs well, putting aside 2 tablespoons for glazing.

To the beaten eggs add sugar, cinnamon or vanilla, olive oil, and the flour previously sifted with baking powder. Add milk and knead lightly. Take a chunk and roll into strips ¼ inch in diameter. Cut and shape into circles about 2 inches in diameter, into pretzel shapes, or any patterns desired. Brush with egg and sprinkle with sesame seeds. Place in pan, lightly oiled and sprinkled with flour. Bake in oven preheated to 350°F. till cookies are crisp and a light brown. MAKES ABOUT 4 DOZEN COOKIES.

Sesame Candy

15 almonds cut in half
½ pound sesame seeds
7 ounces honey
2 tablespoons sugar
½ teaspoon lemon juice

In a saucepan lightly toast the almonds and a few moments later add the sesame seeds and toast lightly. Add honey and sugar, increasing the heat. After the entire mixture comes to a boil reduce heat. Continue to cook, adding the lemon juice gradually and stirring the mixture. After 8 to 10 minutes, or when the mixture has the texture of a heavy sauce, turn off the heat and cover.

When mixture is lukewarm pour on a 12-inch plate dipped in tepid water. Smooth out mixture by patting with spatula. Cut into 1½-inch squares and separate. Let cool and harden. Transfer into tin or jar for use when wanted. MAKES ABOUT 40 PIECES OF CANDY.

Almond and Honey Balls
[*Pinionati*: *"Dainty Fingertips"*]

TURKEY

Caution! Although this delicious and popular holiday confection is easy to prepare, there is a superstition that nobody dare look at the contents of the pot while they are cooking!

Grandmother Gioia unwittingly outraged our loyal and eager maid, Stella, when to avert an unwanted eye and intrusion she instinctively lifted the corner of her apron from her round, motherly body, to shield the pot of bubbling honey from the destructive glance of an onlooker. The most expert Smyrna cook will not defy tradition!

It required all my pleading and the invocation of folklore and anthropology to convince the maid that this gesture was not intended to insult or repulse her but merely to protect the mixture from failure.

Years later, when making the confection myself, I realized the value of this tradition. Actually any distraction may be responsible for lowering the temperature of the mixture, thus spoiling the texture of the candy.

Obey the tradition!

¼ pound almonds
4 to 6 heaping tablespoons flour
2 eggs, beaten with ¾ teaspoon baking
   powder
1 tablespoon olive oil (approximately)
1 pound honey

Place almonds in saucepan and heat till lightly browned. Pour honey over almonds and let heat gradually. In a bowl add enough flour to the beaten eggs to make a soft dough. Add olive oil and knead it into mixture.

Take pieces of dough and roll into strips ½ inch in diameter. Slice off ¼-inch pieces and toss into hot honey mixture. Repeat until all the dough has been so divided. Cook briskly for 20 minutes. Stir to distribute almonds. When the little dough balls are brown the confection is finished. Place on platter. Before serving, warm platter over hot water. SERVES 8.

Beverages

Cherry Punch [*Vishnada*]

  1 pound sour red cherries
  ¾ pound granulated sugar
  1 cup water
     Juice of 1 large lemon

Wash cherries and remove stems. Put all ingredients in a saucepan and bring to a boil. Lower heat and let simmer for 5 minutes until well blended. Transfer to a jar. Let cool and refrigerate. Serve a tablespoonful in a glass of cold water. SERVES 25.

Wine Drink [*Sangria*]

In Andalucía wine diluted with cold water is served with meals when the weather is warm.

  3 cups dry red wine
  1 lemon, cut in slices
  3 cups water
     Ice cubes
     Sugar to taste

Mix ingredients together in a glass pitcher. Serve cold with the meal.

Peach Drink [*Limonada Verbenera*]

  1 bottle red wine
  2 cups cold water
  ½ pound peaches, peeled and thinly sliced
  ⅓ to ½ cup sugar
  1 lemon, sliced
  2 cups ice cubes

Place all ingredients in a bowl or pitcher. Stir with a spoon and let stand one hour. Shortly before serving add ice cubes. Serve in glasses. SERVES 8.

Coffee and Tea

"How?" asked the lovely blonde Russian actress. "How do you make tea with such a fine aroma?"

Likewise, an American guest delighted with the coffee inquires: "What type of coffee do you use; how do you prepare it?"

Our "secret" is freshly boiled water, and exact measurements. The explanation given is that the free oxygen in freshly boiled water produces the best flavor. On the other hand, water which has been boiled too long before using has lost its free oxygen content, tastes stale, and produces a flat-tasting beverage.

American Coffee

> 3 cups water (this equals 4 serving cups)
> 4 heaping tablespoons coarsely ground coffee

Bring water to a boil quickly. Place basket containing coffee in pot. As soon as percolating begins adjust heat to maintain brisk percolating and note time. Allow 2 minutes for each serving cup. Serve immediately or transfer to a glass carafe. Keep coffee warm but do not let it boil. SERVES 4.

Turkish Coffee

> 1½ cups water
> 2 teaspoons sugar
> 4 tablespoons finely pulverized coffee

Measure water into small, heavy saucepan. Add sugar and bring to a boil. Stir in the coffee. Allow brew to froth up three times, turning it down each time; then remove from heat. Add a few drops of cold water. Spoon some of the foam into each cup and pour in the coffee. Each cup must have some of this creamy foam, which in Arabic is called "the face of the coffee." SERVES 4.

Tea

Tea carefully prepared, i.e., brewed or steeped, has a rich amber color and a flavor that delights. Even a tea bag, when brewed, yields a richer and more interesting flavor.

A small teapot is best for brewing. If none is available use a cup and cover with a saucer. Scald the pot. Use a teaspoon of tea for each cup desired. Cover leaves with boiling water. Let brew 3 to 5 minutes. To serve, pour 2 to 3 teaspoons of this essence into each cup. Then add boiling water.

A spot of milk or cream may be added, but the fine flavor of tea should not be neutralized.

Menus

Lunch Menus

Halved Tomato with
    Oregano
Spinach or Leek Pie
Sliced Banana and Ice
    Cream

Cucumber Relish with
    Bread Dressing
Spinach with Rice and
    Cheese
Fruit Cup

Mixed Green Salad
Chicken Livers
Rice Pilaf, Greek Style
Stewed Quince

Green Bean Salad and
    Hard-Cooked Eggs
Stuffed Grape Leaves
Feta Cheese, Yoghurt

Turkish Salad
Eggs, Cuban Style
Rice Pilaf, Greek Style
Strawberries with Orange
    Juice

Gazpacho
Poached Fish with
    Olive Oil Mayonnaise
Custard with Caramel
    Sauce

Honeydew Melon
Eggs Poached in Tomato
    Sauce
Rice Pudding

Fish Soup
Rice Pilaf, Greek Style
Mixed Green Salad
Watermelon Wedges

Fennel and Ripe Olives
Tomato Pie
Compote, Athenian Style

Lettuce and Endive Salad
Spaghetti with Butter
Apricot Whip

Tossed Salad
Eggplant and Ricotta
    Cheese
Orange Jello with Assorted
    Fruit

Dinner Menus

Spinach Pie
Buttered Carrots
Green Olives
Lamb Stew with Baby
    Okra
Bulgur
Pears, Roman Style

Calf's Brains Vinaigrette
Endive Salad
Veal and Mushrooms
Wide Green Beans with
    Herbs
Vermicelli
Compote, Athenian Style

Vegetable Soup
Meat Balls and Parsley à la
    Smyrna
Vermicelli
Broccoli with Lemon and
    Olive Oil Dressing
Date Whip

Anchovies and Pimientos
    on Toast
Tossed Salad
Beef Kebab
Green Beans with Tomato
    Sauce
Rice Pilaf, Greek Style
Compote, Athenian Style

Turkish Salad
Stuffed Zucchini
Chicken Andaluz
Peas and Pods
Vermicelli
Blackberry Sponge

Dandelion Leaves
Lamb Stew with Baby
    Okra
Rice with Chick Peas
Baklava (purchased)

Calamata Olives
Tossed Salad
Beef Kebab
Green Beans with Tomato
    Sauce
Bulgur
Date Whip

Artichokes, Smyrna Style
Blanquette of Veal à la
    Tunis
Peas and Pods
Rice Pilaf, Greek Style
Strawberries with Orange
    Juice

Hearts of Fennel and
    Celery
Spaghetti in Casserole, with
    Meat
Boiled Spinach with Lemon
    and Olive Oil Dressing
Stewed Pears

Mixed Tossed Salad
Herbed Lamb
Casserole of Vegetables
Rice Pilaf, Greek Style
Stewed Quince or Baklava

Eggplant à la Smyrna
Roast Chicken, Spanish
    Style
Green Beans with Tomato
    Sauce
White Rice with Persian
    Garnish
Apricot Meringue

Spinach Stalks Vinaigrette
Watercress and Romaine
    Salad
Fried Brains with Olive Oil
    Mayonnaise
Red Rice topped with
    Fresh or Canned Peas
Apple Pie

Greek Fish Roe
Tomatoes, Onion, and
    Parsley
Greek Olives
Stewed Shoulder Lamb
    Chops, Smyrna Style
White Rice with Turkish
    Dressing
Fruit Cup with Sherry

Buffet or Party Menus

Anchovies, Assorted Olives
Tomatoes with Oregano
Chicken with Rice
Mixed Green Salad
Cookies

Greek Salad
Shish Kebab
Rice Pilaf, Greek Style
Persian Melon

Feta Cheese
Stuffed Grape Leaves
Zucchini Casserole
Red Rice
Seedless Grapes and Sesame
    Seed Cookies

Celery, Olives, Green
    Pepper Rings
Broiled Eggplant and
    Ricotta Cheese
Vermicelli
Lettuce Salad
Apricot Whip

Cucumber with French
    Dressing
Lettuce Salad
Sliced Fish (Halibut),
    Smyrna Style
Vermicelli
Strawberries with Orange
    Juice

Cold Weather Menus

Greek Salad
Lentil Soup
Beef Kebab
Red Rice
Apple Pie

Endive, Olives, Anchovies
Marrow Bean Soup
Veal, North Italian Style
Rice Pilaf
Stewed Prunes

Greek Fish Roe, Olives
Spinach with Beans
Beef Liver in Vinegar Sauce
Rice Pilaf
Pears, Roman Style

Dandelion Leaf Salad
Onions and Chick Peas
Red Rice
Compote, Athenian Style

Artichokes, Smyrna Style
Baked Whole Fish, Smyrna
    Style
Spaghetti in Casserole, with
    Meat
Tomatoes, Green Peppers,
    and Onion
Fruit Cup

Escarole Salad
Stuffed Green Peppers
Green Beans with Tomato
    Sauce
Vermicelli
Apricot Meringue

Warm Weather Menus

These menus can be prepared in advance.

Cucumber Vinaigrette
Beef Patties with Celery
    Leaves
Zucchini Provençal
Vermicelli
Watermelon Wedges

Endive and Romaine Salad
Poached Bass with Parsley
    and Onion Sauce
Asparagus with Lemon and
    Olive Oil Dressing
Potatoes with Onions à la
    Smyrna
Compote, Athenian Style

Tomato with Oregano
Blanquette of Chicken
Celery and Almonds
Rice Pilaf, Greek Style
Pineapple Cubes with Mint

Sorrel Soup
Sliced Fish (Porgy),
    Smyrna Style
Browned Potatoes
Custard with Caramel
    Sauce

Cucumber Relish with
    Bread Dressing
Black Olives
Carrot Sticks
Stuffed Tomatoes
Toasted Fettuccine in
    Tomato Sauce
Stewed Peaches

Glossary of Cooking Terms

BAKE To cook in an oven.

BASTE To moisten food while cooking by pouring over it melted fat, oil or other liquid.

BLANCH To whiten or scald by plunging into boiling water and then into cold.

BOIL To cook in water or liquid that is mostly water, at boiling temperature (212°F.).

BRAISE To sear in fat or hot oil, then cook in covered pan with small amount of liquid.

BROIL To cook by direct heat on a rack placed under the source of heat or over an open fire.

DEEP-FRY To cook in a deep kettle in enough fat to cover or float food.

DREDGE To coat lightly with flour.

FRENCH-FRY See DEEP-FRY.

FRICASSEE To stew pieces of meat, poultry, or game in a little liquid, and serve with a thickened gravy.

FRY To cook in fat or oil without water or cover.

GRILL See BROIL.

MARINATE To let food stand in a liquid (usually a mixture of oil and vinegar or lemon juice) to add flavor or become more tender.

PAN-FRY To cook in a small amount of fat, up to ½ inch, in a frying pan.

PARBOIL To boil until food is partly cooked.

REDUCE To cook a stock briskly until it acquires a heavier consistency.

SCALD To heat liquid to just below boiling point.

SAUTÉ See PAN-FRY.

SIMMER To cook in liquid just below the boiling point at temperatures of 185° to 210°F. Bubbles form slowly and break below the surface.

STEAM To cook food over boiling water in a covered container or in a perforated pan, or on a rack.

STEW To cook in a small amount of liquid, covered, at a low temperature. Meats are stewed at simmering temperature.

Index

The Home of

DENSE GROWTH ▬▬ MODERATE

ADAPTED FROM MAP BY ABNER DIAMOND IN THE 1951

Atlantic Ocean

FRANCE

ITALY

SPAIN

CORSICA

BALEARIC
ISLES

SARDI

SPANISH
MOROCCO

Mediterranean   Sea

FRENCH
MOROCCO

ALGERIA

LIBY